The Mountain In You

Stories and Poetry That Inspire Hope and Purpose For Living

WILLIAM STEPHENSON, PHD

The Mountain In You
Copyright © 2024 by William Stephenson, PhD

ISBN: 979-8895311219 (sc)
ISBN: 979-8895311226 (e)

All rights reserved. No part of this publication may be reproduced, distributed, or transmitted in any form or by any means, including photocopying, recording, or other electronic or mechanical methods, without the prior written permission of the publisher and/or the author, except in the case of brief quotations embodied in critical reviews and other noncommercial uses permitted by copyright law.

The views expressed in this book are solely those of the author and do not necessarily reflect the views of the publisher, and the publisher hereby disclaims any responsibility for them.

Writers' Branding
(877) 608-6550
www.writersbranding.com
media@writersbranding.com

Contents

Preface i
Judgment and Light 1
Resentments 3
A Legacy 5
Limits 7
The Gift of Staying 9
Because of Mary - A Christmas Poem 11
Will There Be Enough? 15
A Running Father 17
Raising The White Flag 21
A Waiting Father 23
Family 25
Learning to Let Go 27
Mysterious Grace 29
An Unexpected Lesson 31
Unfinished 33
Kindergarten 35
One of Those Days 37
When Bread Is Enough 39
The Fear of Abandonment 41
Timing 43
This Moment of Recovery 45
Jersey Boy 47
A Gift To Self 53
Gift to Self 57
Unspoken Love Story 59
Gratitude 63
And So It Goes 65
Fishing With Bread 67

Living In A Waiting Room	69
The Art of Waiting	71
Listening To My Heart	73
Our Lonely Self	77
A Room Without a View	79
A Dead Stump	81
In The Heart	83
The Pure in Heart	85
To Be A Child Again	87
Christal With an "I"	89
Choices I	91
What Are You In For?	93
On Holy Ground	95
I Was Wrong	97
Sanity Is Where You Find It	99
A Recurring Nightmare	101
Where Do I Go?	103
Panic	105
Panic And A Peaceful Heart	107
On Falling	111
Freedom From Fear	113
The Consequences of Anger	117
The Power of Forgiveness	119
How Far?	121
A Second Look	123
Lessons	125
Mitigating Circumstances	127
Requirements	129
A Test of Wills	131
Grudges	133
An Unassembled Peace	135
Justification	139
An Awakened Soul	141
Free to Believe	143
My Resource	145

As My Day Begins 147
Beginnings 149
On Finishing 151
A Need For An Ending 153
An Epilogue: *The Storyteller*.. 155

Preface

As I watch this book get close to publication, I am celebrating my 79th birthday, and I ponder if this may be my last book. Writing is easy; publishing is what ages me. My wife, Carol, deserves more from me than six hours in my office each day/night, writing.

But it was that kind of thinking that generated the contents of this book. I wanted to have a book of what I judged to be my best poetry and also the stories that gave me the most inspiration and motivation to be open to a new client.

I have already written a book that captures my journey with prayer and poetry: **Sunrises & Sunsets: A Daily Journal of Renewal, Redemption, and Rejoicing**. But now comes this book that reflects my love of free verse and my dance with human drama. The stories I have chosen to be the most helpful to me will surprise some people. More than half of the twenty-six stories have nothing to do with dying, but they are stories of people who gave me so much courage and confidence.

I am grateful to so many of my clients who would often ask what I was writing about, and then, sharing that with them, we would often work on it together, and it would carry us into a deeper understanding and growth.

Whether this is my last or the launching pad for another, read it in such a way that you could be sitting beside me, and together, we wrote something that could also reveal a little more light to guide your way.

—Bill Stephenson

Judgment and Light

Go into a dark room and turn on the light.
The light doesn't create
The dust that is in the air,
It merely reveals it.

Judgment is like that.
Judgment is the light
That shows us what really matters.

Love and Judgment ought not to be related.
But they are.
They need to be spoken
In the same breath.
They come from the same house
And live in the same room.
Love and Judgment seek each other out.

William Stephenson, PhD

"When my wife died,
My whole world came to an end.
What didn't matter were the things
I thought mattered!
Why did I have to wait until the end
To discover what really mattered?"

Recovery
Is not one of darkness
But one of Light.
It is the light,
As in a room once in darkness,
That shows us what really matters.

Recovery is one of Light and Love.
This is the decision that changes my life.
Love and Judgment are connected…
"This is the Judgment
That the Light has come!"

Resentments

It seems that it all starts in the family…
Being-left-out feelings,
Resentful feelings,
Hurtful feelings,
Bad memories.

It all starts with people we trusted.

What is our response?
To become hard or get revenge?
To find a target for the hurt?
To lash out and attack?
Or do we allow ourselves to be healed?

How do we stop
Seeing forgiveness as just an idea
And letting it become an event?

How do we discover that in our lives?

How do we stop punishing ourselves,
And others
For our hurt and pain?

William Stephenson, PhD

I wait upon God.
Listening for the whisper
Of God's command.
That my past has been received.
And my past will not be
A condition for my future.
That I can go from a bad memory
To a good memorial.

I wait upon God,
And seek to be changed and renewed.
To be set free from what has been,
And what might have been
And live for what may be.

A Legacy

She was thirty-seven and the mother of three children. She was troubled because she couldn't seem to want to go back to her childhood home and be with her parents when holidays obligated her. There was a sense of aloofness, distance, and coldness with her mother. But she decided to go and visit her parents.

When she got back to her childhood home, she was in the kitchen with her mother, helping to prepare the family dinner. As she was working with her hands, her head bowed, she began a long-awaited conversation with her mother. A conversation she had rehearsed in therapy several times.

"Mom, when I was a little girl, why didn't you hug me more often? Why didn't you tell me that you loved me? Whenever I would go and stay the night at my girlfriend's house, her mother would come in at night and hug her and squeeze her and stroke her head and tell her she loved her. I was so envious of them. Whenever you came in at night before going to bed, I would wish expectantly for you to hug and kiss me good night, but all you would do was

lay my clothes out for the following day. It's like you were more concerned about what other people were thinking and saying than you were about me."

Her mother, with tears filling her eyes, looked at her daughter and said, *"Oh, my child, didn't you know? Didn't I ever tell you? When I was a little girl, I had to go to school every day wearing dirty, wrinkled clothes. I swore to God, if I should ever have a daughter like you, that would never happen! When I laid your clothes out each night, that was my way of hugging you. That was my way of saying I love you. Didn't you know?"*

For nearly thirty years this daughter held on to this resentment before she had this conversation with her mother, and her mother had not been able to say the words every child hungers to hear on a regular basis: *"I love you."* More than thirty Mother's Days had come and gone with this invisible wedge between them. These two found each other, and Mother's Day would never be the same again. Indeed.

Limits

There is an inescapable aloneness
About life.
Our refusal to accept this
Can cause us to feel all kinds of guilt
When someone else goes to pieces.

We so want
To protect those we love
From the consequences of their
Decisions and their behavior.

It is hard sometimes
To love someone enough
To leave them alone.
Even if it feels like abandonment
To the other person.

The message found in Recovery is...
"You can carry the message
But you can't carry the person."

We cannot protect our loved ones
From suffering.
Each of us must bear the consequence
For our own decisions and action.

Our hope comes
When we can accept these limits.
Then we can use our energy to do
The things we can for our loved ones.

William Stephenson, PhD

If we will walk
With each other
When we can.
Then we can stand
Alone
When we must.

The Gift of Staying

"You are before this court to determine whether you are capable of parenting your child. The state has issued a request to take custody of your child because of your physical handicap. How do you plead?" asked the judge.

This is where Jacqueline's story begins. Yet the beginning and end of her story are tightly connected.

The scene in the court room took place thirty-one years ago. Jacqueline appeared in court with her five-month old son. The context of the State's complaint was that Jacqueline was born without any arms or legs. They could find no justification for someone that handicapped being the primary parent of a child. She was confined to a motorized wheel chair she could maneuver with her breath. Otherwise, she needed total care just like her baby.

However, no one in that courtroom knew of her determination and character. She was there to fight for her right and responsibility to raise her son, Steven. Her lawyer presented several character witnesses, all advocating on Jacqueline's behalf.

Then it was Jacqueline's turn to speak or testify to her ability to retain custody of her child. Jacqueline requested permission to demonstrate her ability instead of speaking about it. With her primary care-giver, the three of them proceeded to the center of the courtroom where a changing table was placed for all the powers to see.

Jacqueline then proceeded to undress and redress her infant son by using only her lips and tongue! She did all this in record time, talking to Steven throughout the demonstration. She kissed him and then turned to the judge and said, *"I had not planned on getting pregnant, your honor, but I beg of you not to turn this unplanned birth into a tragedy for me and my son. I am a good person and I am determined, with the help of my care-givers, to be an exemplary parent to Steven. Your honor, please don't take Steven from me. Please don't take Steven from his mother."*

The judge sat in silence for a significant amount of time, just looking at Jacqueline. Finally, he said, *"Never in my courtroom have I witnessed a more courageous act of love and commitment. Ms. Smith, I am so sorry that you were asked to defend the competency of your parental rights. I admonish* the State Department of Welfare for ever bringing this to my court. I award you complete custody of your child and can only hope that the two of you will find your future to be a hopeful one. Case dismissed."

It was her son who would tell of their beginning of a life together. He said, "Our life together was not easy. I grew up fast and I was often my mom's primary care-giver. When I wanted to go out and play or participate in a group like the Boy Scouts, or a school activity, instead I was home taking care of my mom. There were times when I resented that obligation. But, today, I now appreciate the devotion we both had to make our relationship work."

He said, "She wants me to go home and take care of my wife and son. But, I'm staying here beside her until the end. She is the one who taught me that. Stay. Hang in there. Don't give up. I can only hope my son will learn that from me."

He was a man of his word. He stayed by his mother's side in the hospice day after day, night after night until she died. He was not going to allow this woman of character, integrity and selfless love die alone. She died on Christmas Eve. It was a good death. Now, all is calm.

Because of Mary - A Christmas Poem

Because of Mary,
All class,
All castes,
All hierarchical systems are now undermined.

Because of Mary,
The world can no longer categorize someone
As being worthless
Or worth less than somebody else.

Because of Mary,
The Christmas story is for little ones and the poor...
The victims of bigotry and bullying...
All who are looked down upon,
All from whom less is expected, and, therefore,
Less is given.

William Stephenson, PhD

Because of Mary,
The reign of numbers is at an end.
The reign of statistics is finished.
The reign of seeing the world's population
As "objective projections" is over.

Because of Mary,
Nobody is an "it" and,
Everybody is a "you!"
The reign has begun
That every person is precious!

Because of Mary,
God says that Jesus
Isn't the reason for the season.
God says you and I
Are the reason for the season!
We are all the reason!
No one is left out!

Because of Mary,
Christmas is for those who are
Oppressed,
Rejected,
Neglected,
Forgotten.

Because of Mary,
Christmas is for the
Nobody's,
The cyphers,
The non-persons.
All of those judged to be
The great misery in this world.

The Mountain In You

Because of Mary,
Christmas isn't just about Jesus…
Christmas is also about
The poor,
The "lowly",
The least
In this world.

Because of Mary,
God has knocked
The queen and the king
Down to size
And put a Nobody
On the throne.
So that the world
Will now proclaim:
"Blessed are you among women."

And Mary
Comes this Christmas,
Not riding on a donkey,
But in a twenty-five year old
Broken-down Buick,
Driven by her chronically
Unemployed boyfriend.

You can pick her out…
You know what she looks like…
You've seen her,
Haven't you?
Holding a cardboard sign
On the street corner?

William Stephenson, PhD

Surely...
You have seen her.

So,

Brace yourself!
There's a birthquake coming!

Because of Mary.

Will There Be Enough?

How do we confront our fear
That tomorrow
There will be enough?

How do we get through that feeling
That our spouse has never loved us enough?
That our children have never loved us enough?
That no one has ever loved us enough?

How do we find freedom and release from
The resentments
The disappointments
The disillusionments
In our relationships?

How do we stop hanging on to those
Issues in our lives?

We all have an appointment with death.
What we give away before that appointment
Is what we leave behind.

William Stephenson, PhD

A Running Father

Oh
The expectations we have of our children,
The expectations we have as parents on ourselves!

Who
Do we want love from
More than our children?

Who
Can hurt us
More than our children?

It's
The one relationship that
Once it's started
Will never change.

No
Matter what happens
You can never cease
To be a dad or a mom
A daughter or a son.

But
Oh the pain of alienation
Misunderstanding,
Separation
From a child or a parent.
It's so deep and never-ceasing.

What to do?
What to say?
How does the healing begin?
Who initiates?
How do we respond?

William Stephenson, PhD

Do we hand them a list of conditions
Or just offer them our love?

As parents
Do we sit with our pride
Thinking of what we expect
Our child must do
To earn back our love?

Or
Stand and peer off into the horizon…
"Is it? Could it be?"

And then,
Run!
Throw our arms around them!
Kiss them!
Throw a party!
Shout to the heavens,
"You're home!"

We
Live our lives too often in fear.
Afraid that we have missed the boat.
Afraid that we have failed those we hold dear.
Afraid that we have even failed God.

And so
We run and hide
In strange, far off places:
Behind smiles we don't feel,
Behind demands we can't meet,
Behind tasks we can't accomplish,
Behind expectations we can't achieve.

We
Are afraid
Because we have forgotten
Who we are...
Whose we are.

We
Need to remember once again
That we are Parented
By the One who seeks us.
By the One who moves within us.
By the One who wants us home again.
By the One who wants us to be free again.

William Stephenson, PhD

Raising The White Flag

A colleague of mine decided to take the train up along the west coast of California to attend a conference. A soldier sitting across the aisle was on his way back to his barracks near Monterey. He noticed that the young soldier seemed rather anxious and decided to speak to him, saying, *"Looks like something's bothering you. Do you want to talk about it?"*

The young man quickly turned and said, *"Yes!"* He explained that he used to live on a ranch that the train would soon pass. A few years ago, he'd had a terrible quarrel with his father, and it ended with him vowing to never return home again.

He said, *"I've been gone now for three years. I drop a note every once in a while to my mom, but I haven't been back. I really want to go back home, so before leaving for this trip, I wrote a letter to my mom telling her that I would be coming by on the train, and it would stop at the station for a brief moment. Talk to dad and if it's all right with him, if he doesn't mind me stopping by, just hang something white out in front of the house, and I'll get off the train. But, if it isn't okay with Dad, and I don't see anything white hanging out, I'll understand and keep going.'"*

The soldier then said, *"Sir, we're almost there. It's just around the next curve, and I'm afraid to look. Would you look for me?"*

My colleague peered out the window as the train turned the corner and then gently urged the soldier to look out the window too. When he did, he couldn't even see the farmhouse! His father and mother had tied together two white bed sheets and had them flying from the flag pole. They had draped their house with everything white. They had white bed sheets, a white bedspread, a white tablecloth and white towels covering the front of the house!

The last time he saw that young soldier, he had his duffle bag and he was running across the field and to home.

This Teachable Moment reminds us that recovery asks us to let go of our hurt and pride and to wave the white flag that proclaims, *"Let's Find A Way To Start A New Journey."* May it be so.

William Stephenson, PhD

A Waiting Father

I remember when I was eight years old. The second oldest of four boys. We lived in a rural area of western New York. It was a wonderful place to grow up. We lived on a lake, there were four seasons, we had a boat, and my dad was a well-known fisherman and boat man in the area. We did so much together. I adored my father.

One day, after school, about four o'clock, I asked my father if I could go up the street and play with some friends. He said it would be fine but to remember that dinner was at six o'clock and I had better not be late. He said that while looking directly at me, and I sensed he wasn't kidding. The message was clear. Don't be late!

I lost track of the time. When the sun was setting I realized it was well past the time I was expected to be home. I asked my friend's mother what time it was, and she said it was 6:20. I raced out of the house and ran down the street toward home. As I neared my home, there standing in the middle of the street was my father with his hands on his hips. I knew I was in serious trouble.

I stopped running because I was crying so hard. I had let my father down, and I knew I was going to be punished for not keeping my word. As I neared my father, my crying turned to sobbing. I was so afraid of what the consequences were going to be.

When I reached my father, I sobbed, *"Daddy, I didn't mean to be late. I'm sorry. I'm so sorry!"*

He knelt down, pulled me into his arms, and held me until I stopped crying. Then he said,

"Son, you have punished yourself more than I would have ever punished you. You're home now, and I'm just glad that you are safe."

He held me in his arms and took me home to dinner. No allowance for two weeks!

I didn't know then I would have this hero in my life for only seven more years. My father would be diagnosed with a rare disease that would take five years to kill him. I would eventually become his primary caregiver. While my mother had to work, and when my father was out of remission, I would be the one to bathe him, light his cigarettes, make sure his paperwork for his business was in order, and stay with him for hours to make sure he was safe.

Little did I know I was being trained to become a caregiver to those who were soon to die. Little did I know my father would become my first patient.

Family

Why is it that the conflict
We experience in our families
Is more confronting of us
Than any conflict
We ever experience anywhere else?

Why is it that it is in the family
Where we will experience
Both passionate love
And hostile hate?

It seems that the family
Is the most intimate setting
In which we have to learn
How to be fit to live with.

Yet,
The lessons of such love and family
Are being taught by teachers
Who are themselves pupils.

We
Learn about hypocrisy from hypocrites!

We
Learn about forgiveness from people
Who are still learning how to forgive!

It is in the family
Where people really know who we are.

It is in the family
Where people will love us
In spite of ourselves,
Not because of...

Perhaps
That is why Jesus
Described the family
As a model for the Kingdom of God...
Full of conflict and hypocrisy...

That
God loves us still.
In spite of...

Learning to Let Go

Hell found me. That's how I felt when I was fourteen. My father had been stricken with a very rare disease. For two years he would battle that disease and being the oldest son in the house, I became his primary care-giver. My life as a teenager was over. Taking care of my dad became my life and because this disease often left him delirious and he became unmanageable, my life became a living hell.

I helped him with his baths and going to the bathroom. I dressed him, lit his cigarettes, did all of his office files and made sure he kept his appointments with clients when he was well enough. But when he was very ill, I refused to leave his side. School be damned.

He died suddenly when I was just sixteen. I had a very difficult time accepting my father's death. I stoically hid my pain from everyone and as for God? I blamed God for making my father suffer and our family suffer. Hell not only found me but my entire family. We were destitute and missing a wonderful father. Thus, because of the living Hell I felt I was living in, I made everyone around me as miserable as I felt.

Two years later, after graduating from high school, my family moved from Chautauqua, New York to Southern California. But I went back that first Christmas to spend it with my childhood friends. While I was there, I decided to visit my father's grave. I had not done so since his burial nearly two years before.

Unfortunately, there had been a tremendous snow storm and the huge cemetery that my father had been buried in was impossible to drive into, let alone find his marker, just six inches above the ground. But I was determined. I began trudging through the cemetery in the deep snow, vaguely recalling that he was buried in our family plot which was located somewhere across the veteran's section, which I also could not find. Too much snow! Again, I felt as if Hell had found me. And then, as if a strange force were guiding me, I found myself kneeling down in the snow and digging with my bare hands. And there before me was my father's gravestone.

Cold and wet and exhausted, for I was there for a long time, I began to pray for the first time in two years. And with tears in my eyes, I gave thanks to God for who my father was and what he had meant to me and what I hoped to become.

I then took some snow and covered up his gravestone again. And I prayed, *"He's yours now, Lord. He's all yours."* I then knew that I was free from that Hell and I was free to enjoy the memories of those sixteen years that we had shared together. And by re-covering his gravestone, I was honoring my father. I had discovered my past and then I moved on.

I learned how to help others honor their dead. Remember them? Yes. Share our memories about them with each other? Yes. And then put them in God's hands and move on.

Mysterious Grace

It has taken a long time
For me to learn that I can't be
All things to all people.
I can't bring wholeness and wellness
To everyone I counsel.

It has taken a long time
To come to a place of calm
And know that I am
Often going to fail many
Who have trusted me with their
Remaining days of life and
They will end it with still too
Much turmoil and heartbreak.
My dream for them will go unfilled.
Their relationships will continue to be fractured.

It has taken a long time,
But I am learning
To make peace with my ghosts,
Those that I could not help
So that I can become better prepared
For others I hope I can.

It's an act of grace, actually.
I think it's a mysterious grace.

That is...
God's purpose for me is greater
Than my ability to screw things up!
Whether I am a success or a failure,
People who entrust me with their lives
Are so beautiful,
So full of wisdom and grace.

They are such teachers of
What is important and
What is important, really.
They just seem to know how short
Life really is.

To have peace within is to embrace that
"God isn't done with you yet!
When God made you
He knew what He was doing!"

It's a mysterious grace.

An Unexpected Lesson

A woman, named Margaret, who had been battling cancer for a long time, asked me, the hospice counselor, to come and help her die. Margaret would not have lasted as long as she had if it had not been for her positive attitude on life. Her whole being was filled with hope and she extended her life because of her hope and because of the love her family surrounded her with each day.

Margaret had such a grateful spirit and one of the truths she believed is that hope doesn't produce gratitude. Most of us think that's what is going to happen. If we can be hopeful then we will be grateful. Margaret believed that it's the other way around. It is gratitude that produces hope. She was so grateful for her family who surrounded her and that filled her with hope. She loved her life even to the very end.

But she grew tired and her loved ones questioned, *"Why can't she get well again?"* And the answer came to all who were around her: *"Sometimes our loved ones have to die in order to get well."*

Death is not always a dark messenger. Sometimes it's an angel of light. Sometimes at the end of the spiritual journey of birth to death we have to trust that God's gift of death is a miracle that brings new life. I couldn't help Margaret to die, but she taught me much about how to live.

William Stephenson, PhD

Unfinished

There was a time when
My life was consumed with guilt.
The goal in my life was to find
A way to deal with a boat-load of guilt.
It had control of all parts of my life.

There was a time when
My life was one big "Let's Make a Deal."
If only I would believe a certain way
Then all of my depression,
Fears, failures and frustrations
Would go away.
It was an "If-Then" way of living.
But God wouldn't keep his end of the bargain
And I became an angry, vengeful person.

There came that moment
In my life when I experienced life as a gift.
That I am loved, warts and all.
I didn't have to be lovable to be loved.
I didn't have to be guilt-free
To be acceptable.
I didn't have to work day and night
To earn forgiveness.

William Stephenson, PhD

Kindergarten

I am learning
some of the most precious moments
I have
are when I give myself and those near me
the time to listen very carefully.
Sometimes I wonder
if I live life too cautiously,
share my faith too stingily,
administer my commitments from a medicine dropper,
make my offerings from my leftovers.

William Stephenson, PhD

Too often I live
from a frightened spirit
rather than a generous heart.
Why do I choose to live my life out of a scarcity concept?
I give of myself to others as if I have to give up something.

I am learning
that I give as I receive.
When I feel abundant love and abundant grace,
then I give the same way.
I give to others from an expression of my compassion.

I need to remember
that the only thing I take beyond the grave
is what I release before I go there.

One of Those Days

Several years ago, when my children were still very young, I had had one of those days. Everything that could go wrong, did. And, I had appointments with people that night.

I came home and dinner was getting ready, so I went into the living room and I picked up the newspaper and I put it around me as if it was some sort of a curtain or wall, indicating to anybody who passed by, that they just better keep going.

I had been sitting there in this stew for awhile when suddenly I saw some legs at my feet. I peeked around my newspaper and there was my four year old son, Jon. He looked up under the paper and he said, *"Daddy, you wanna go outside?"* And I said, *"No, not right now. Perhaps later."* I went back to my curtain.

A few minutes later I felt him nudge at my foot again. He had crawled up under the newspaper. He said, *"Daddy, would you like to go play catch?"*

I had been a father long enough to know that he wanted more from me than to just go outside and play catch. I was in no mood to work out what he wanted and then to debate with him why he wasn't going to have it.

I flippantly responded to him by saying, *"Jon, why don't you go watch Sesame Street, or go tease your sister, whatever is more appropriate."* I went back behind my paper curtain, thinking that I had successfully been able to outwit his needs or his wants.

I don't remember when I became aware of my son, but I was aware of his presence because somehow, this little boy had crawled up onto the couch, placed himself underneath my newspaper and fallen asleep on my lap with his arms around me.

I put my newspaper down and held and hugged my son. I bathed in that sacred moment. Awareness stabbed my consciousness. My perception of a bad day--all the people I had to deal with--and my suspicions, had kept me from experiencing what my son was trying--not to take from me--but to give to me.

It was one of those days.

William Stephenson, PhD

When Bread Is Enough

In one hospital filled with refugee children, the nursing staff discovered that in spite of the fact the children were well fed and cared for, when bedtime came, the war-torn and orphaned children would begin to toss and turn, unable to fall asleep, as they were too afraid.

The staff psychologist soon discovered that these children were remembering how in the past they were often going to bed alone and hungry and would have to wake up alone and hungrier. In the depths of their subconscious, they were fighting sleep because they did not want to experience that hunger again.

The staff psychologist instructed the nurses to give each of the children a slice of bread when they went to bed. The children were told not to eat the piece of bread they were given. If they were still hungry, they could go and get some other food at the nurses station. That particular piece of bread, however, they were to just hold onto to and try to go to sleep.

It worked. When they were sure in the very depths of their being that tomorrow there would be enough, slowly but surely, the children fell peacefully asleep.

The teachable moment is knowing that children, and perhaps we adults, can know peace when we have the confidence that our basic needs are not threatened from being taken away or from lack of resources. Wholeness and wellness calls for us to be able to thrive as well as survive.

William Stephenson, PhD

The Fear of Abandonment

He was just a young man in his twenties and he was dying of AIDS. It would not be long now. He was frightened and all alone. As his counselor, I was called to see if anything could be done to help the young man.

He was very near death, but he still had the will to fight for every moment of life that was within him.

He shared with me how frightened he was of dying alone. Everyone he knew and loved had abandoned him. He had no one to turn to. No one to comfort him. No one to talk to or feel love from. No one who would even touch him or hold him.

I knew that he was a man of faith, following a Christian journey, and yet no one who shared his faith came to visit him.

He knew, however, that we shared a similar spiritual journey and he began to share about his faith. Immediately I sensed what might help his fear of being so alone and abandoned. I rushed out to the commissary and found a bread roll and brought it back to his room.

He could no longer swallow or take anything by mouth, so I took a piece of the bread, placed it in the palm of his hand, and reminded him how Christ, at the end of his life, offered bread to his disciples, saying to each of them, *"Whenever you break bread together, remember me. Remember that this bread means that I will never abandon you. That even in death, I will always be with you. You will never again be alone."*

That young man understood. He held on to that bread for the rest of that evening, still clinging to it when I had to say goodnight...

He would die a few days later. I was not there when he died. I missed it by just a few minutes, but the nurses told me that he continued to hold on to the bread day and night. That even as they took his body away to the morgue, the piece of bread was clasped tightly in the palm of his hand.

What he is able to teach us, is what he came to know... That surrounding us is a God who will never abandon us, will never let us go.

William Stephenson, PhD

Timing

Sometimes
Things go dead wrong.
There are times when we feel
As if we've just made
Too many mistakes.
So many
That we begin to wonder
If we ourselves are a mistake.

We serve as judge,
Jury and prosecuting attorney.
We condemn ourselves:
"I'll always be lonely."
"I'll always be a mistake."
"I'll always be a failure."
"I will never truly recover."

We suffer
From the fatigue of fate.
We make a short-term verdict
Become a life-long conclusion.
We suffer from hardening
Of our categories.
We feel betrayed
By our hope.

William Stephenson, PhD

To be in the journey of recovery,
Whatever cul-de-sac
We find ourselves...
Whatever the vote against us...
They are all short-term verdicts.

The life-long conclusion is
That God's vote is for us.
Not just for now,
But for always.

This Moment of Recovery

For one
Who has been given
Power I seldom use
And opportunities
I often ignore...
Let this moment of recovery
Be a new beginning.

I need
To be reminded
To not give up
But to grow up.

I cannot
Lose my fears
Until I am willing to face
The things for which I am afraid.

I cannot
Profess a faith
To live by
Until I begin
To really live by faith!

William Stephenson, PhD

In this moment
Of a new beginning of recovery
I need to re-sensitize myself
To God's hope for my life
Lest measuring myself
By the worst I have done
I fail to believe
In what God knows
I can become.

As I accept
This new beginning of recovery
I open myself to the next step
And give my soul the encouragement
To begin again.

Jersey Boy

His name was Anthony. He was nine years old and from Jersey Shores. He was a kid who loved the beach and sand so much that he practically lived there. But he had cancer. Bone cancer. Initially in the spine, it was spreading rapidly. He came out to California to participate in an experimental trial, but his chances were not good. I was asked to be part of his care as a counselor to him and his family.

Anthony liked to draw. That was going to be my way of getting through to him. We started to draw together, almost competitively. But the rule I expected us to follow was to describe or explain what the drawing meant, or how we felt about what we had drawn. We spent several hours drawing and talking with each other about our drawings and about our lives.

"*Dr. Bill, what are you drawing today?*"

"*I'm drawing the house I grew up in. Would you like to see it?*"

"*Why did you draw this house today and not yesterday?*"

"*Anthony, your intuition is incredible. Because today is the day my father died, and I was home at the time I was told of his death. I drew the house today to remember him. Anthony, what would you draw that will help others remember you?*"

He thought about this for several moments, and then he said,

"*I would draw myself running on the beach like I used to before the cancer. I want people to remember me when I was well, not when I was sick.*"

"*Would you draw that for me, Anthony? I've only known you when you've been sick. Would you show me what you were like when you were well?*"

"*Sure! But would you tell me more about your father, Dr. Bill?*"

"*I will, but will you tell me more about how you feel with your battle with cancer? Would you be willing to draw me a picture of that?*"

"*Tomorrow, when you come to see me again, I will have a picture of me and my cancer.*"

"*Fair enough. Now let me tell you about my father.*"

He listened intently as I described my father's life and battle with a rare disease, and how, as a fifteen-year-old, I made the commitment to care for him until his death. Anthony had many questions, and eventually, he began to understand that my relationship with my father was more important than dwelling upon his impending death. Death could never take away the love my father and I had for each other.

"*Dr. Bill, I already have a drawing of me and my cancer. But I was afraid to show it to anyone. I think I can now.*" He pulled out of his dresser drawer a picture. I asked him to describe it to me.

"*This is a picture of a rocket that is just about to crash into a fiery mass of destruction, hurting all those near it.*"

"*I see five people nearby. Is that your mom, dad, and your sister? Who are the other two?*"

"My grandparents."

"And the rocket is you, isn't it?"

"Yes. My cancer isn't just killing me, but it's destroying everyone near me. We were all so happy until I got cancer. It's all my fault!"

Then Anthony leaned against me and wept. And wept. He hadn't cried like this ever before. He felt so responsible for all the sadness and anguish his family was having to endure.

The next day, I called for a family conference and I asked Anthony to share his picture. I told them no one was to leave, no matter how emotional things got to be, and it was indeed a very emotional time. But they listened to him, and Anthony felt they had listened. They talked about their journey with this disease that had attacked their son, her brother, and their grandson. They told the truth. For the first time, everyone was telling each other the truth.

It was a marathon session, and we would have more of them from time to time so they would stay committed to the honesty this nine-year-old said he needed from them.

The last drawing Anthony gave to me was a picture of the ocean with the sun on the horizon. It was a beautiful and colorful picture. And flying around in the sky were five birds all clustered together.

"Are the birds your family, Anthony? And is the sun setting a symbol of you?"

"Yes and no, Dr. Bill. You forget I'm from New Jersey, and, unlike here in California, the sun rises on the ocean's horizon."

"No more rockets crashing, huh, Anthony?"

"No more crashing rockets, Dr. Bill. I'm into sunrises."

Our last session together began with this question: "Anthony," I asked, "you're going home to New Jersey tomorrow. Is there anything you want to talk about before you leave?"

The trials did not work for Anthony; he would be going home without a cure, and what seemed to his family as if all hope was gone. Suddenly, everything seemed to be an ending and they dreaded thinking of a new beginning without Anthony, their son, brother, and grandson.

"When I get home, I want to go to the beach. I know I can't get in the ocean or use my beach board, but I just want to be out there so that I can watch my friends, smell the ocean air and just be a part of the action for as

long as I can. Maybe even build a bonfire when the sun goes down. Do you think my parents would let me? I can't walk but I could be carried or maybe the lifeguards would help with their Jeep. I don't know, I was just thinking."

"Anthony, one way to convince them is to think beyond yourself. Whom would you consider inviting to this event? Who would value being a part of this event with you?"

Together we began to make a list of everyone he wanted to invite. More than forty people ended up on his list.

"Now, Anthony, why do you want these particular people?

"I want to thank them for all of their love and support since I got sick. I want to tell them how much they mean to me."

"Remember the song I taught you and your family to use to remind each other of your commitment to each other?

"I could teach them that song and then they would be part of that commitment! Yeah, that would be so cool!"

"Sounds like we need another family conference, Anthony. Are you up for that? And you need to prepare yourself if they don't support your idea." Remember, you've been thinking about this, but they haven't. You may have to give them some time to get on board. Are you okay with that?"

"I understand, Dr. Bill. But I'm running out of time."

A long silence lingered between us as we just looked at each other. Tears welled up in both of our eyes and a long hug followed. A meeting of the family took place soon after. Anthony presented his project after several rehearsals in front of me. They thought it was a great idea with conditions. His fever had to be low-grade. His pain had to be at a manageable level and there had to be a controlled time of two hours. The weather also had to be user-friendly with low winds. He agreed. Anthony and his family left the next day. Their trip to California had come to an end. But their journey back to New Jersey had a new beginning.

Anthony went home and immediately started planning his beach event. He spent every waking hour when he was strong enough planning, writing invitations, getting help from his friends who now came over to visit with him because they felt so included in the planning. Occasionally, we would Face-Time his meetings about the Bonfire event with his friends and family. He kept me informed through every step of the progress. He expected me to somehow attend. I knew how many like Anthony I was committed to and he understood that they needed me just as he had.

"Dr. Bill, it's really going to happen! Everyone I've sent an invitation to wants to come! Did you get yours?"

"Yes, Anthony and I said I'd try to be there via Facetime."

"Fantastic, Dr. Bill. I'm so excited! This has taken on a life of its own. I have so much hope that this is going to work. Thanks, Dr. Bill, for giving me something to hope in."

"Are you ready to teach them the song, Anthony?"

"Me and the family sing it every night before bedtime. I'm ready and I've printed it out so that everyone will have the words."

The night of the bonfire was a perfect night. Anthony made his "grand entrance" via the lifeguards. All six jeeps in caravan delivered Anthony with cheers and horns. More than sixty people attended, and they were all given an opportunity, if they chose, to share with Anthony and the others how important this event meant to them. I was watching on FaceTime, but Anthony didn't know that I was actually a short distance away observing this wonderful celebration of life.

Then, Anthony asked them to turn to the song sheet they had been given. It was time to close the bonfire celebration. Anthony told them that these words were from the Book of Ruth and the words were Ruth's covenant with her mother-in-law, Naomi. He told them that this was now the covenant he and his family had claimed as theirs and he invited them to be part of their covenant.

As he was about to lead them in song, I began to sing from a distance as I moved toward the circle around the bonfire. He recognized my voice. *"Dr. Bill!"* and struggled to stand out of his chair. He joined me in singing as we embraced along with his family. We sang the song through and then invited everyone to join us.

Wherever you go, I shall go.
Wherever you live, so shall I live.
Your people will be my people,
And your God will be my God too. * (Sung 2-3 times)*

It was a very sacred moment for all of us. This now ten-year-old boy had transformed us all with a new hope and a new beginning. Anthony would die just months later from an unexpected infection with his family all around his hospital bed. They also fulfilled Anthony's request which was to sing their song after he was gone.

Every year, around the date of his death, many of the people who attended the first bonfire, gather at that same place, build a huge bonfire, remember the life of Anthony, and always close with the song that reminds them of their covenant with Anthony and with each other.

When Anthony was told to go home after his medical trials, he felt as if all hope was gone. His life had come to an end. What he discovered was that the only thing that was coming to an end was the trip to California. When he went home to New Jersey, he found a new beginning. He had hope again. He had a reason to fight for every day he could steal from death.

*Lyrics written by Akiva Romer-Segal.
Tune written by Colleen Dauncey

A Gift To Self

Everybody knows
That winning is everything.
But in recovery, one is asked,
"Do you want to really live and be free?
Really?"

The Shakers sing,
"'Tis a gift to be simple,
'Tis a gift to be free."

That is,
Life is a gift
And it comes to us through grace.

A life that has no anxiety about tomorrow,
A life that turns the other cheek,
A life that worships God and not possessions,
A life committed to recovery,
A life not easily achieved.

William Stephenson, PhD

This is a life that learns
What the Shakers sing:
"To bow and bend..."
Whether I am on the winning side
Or on the losing side
Of any "contest."

As I come to a change in my life
I see that many men and women
Are turning to a simpler life,
Discovering that having more
Does not achieve more
Happiness and security.

They are
Simplifying their "wanters,"
Rearranging their values and priorities,
Letting go of their differences and divisions,
"Coming down where they ought to be."

People in recovery
Remind me
That when we exalt ourselves
We break harmony with God's creation.

On this day of reflection
The gift I give myself is
To live more simply.
To have the courage to trust.
To believe that my life is good just as it is.
To trust that God's grace is sufficient for me.
To trust that life is buoyant
And there is something surrounding me
And holding me up.

So that I can
"Go and come down in this world
Where I ought to be…"
Trusting grace
As a bird trusts the air.

Trusting
In God's grace that way
May not make me feel safer,
But I'll be freer.
I will be on the way to wholeness,
To recovery.

William Stephenson, PhD

Gift to Self

There are days
I need to stop,
check my address,
to know who I am,
and whose I am.

To find again the secret to the journey.

When I feel frayed, frazzled and frightened,
When I am hurting, hassled and hungry,
I must remember that what I search for,
is a gift I already have within me,
waiting to be re-discovered.

William Stephenson, PhD

Unspoken Love Story

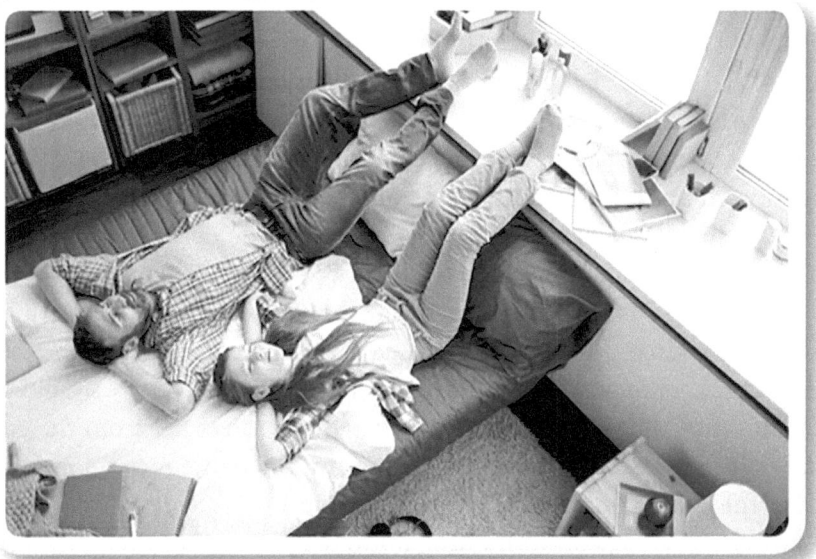

Carolyn was just sixteen. She had an advanced form of cancer that was weakening her more every day. Alan was twenty-three. His cancer was just as advanced and was also weakening his ability to thrive. Carolyn was from the deep South; Alan was from New York City. Carolyn had two very committed and protective parents, and Alan was alone and had no support system.

They came to try an experimental cancer treatment regimen they hoped would give them more time. But, by the time they arrived, the doctors had told them their cancer was too far along and they would not be accepted as candidates to participate in the drug trials. Unfortunately, they were both so weak it was necessary to keep them in the hospital and provide them with palliative care. That's when I was called in to assist them and Carolyn's family. Their rooms were on the same floor and hallway.

Initially, both of them were able to get out of bed, and with wheelchairs, they were able to leave their rooms. They met each other in the hall as their wheelchairs gently ran into each other. It was love at first sight. For the next two weeks, they were nearly inseparable. They ate together, spent long hours in the patients' lounge, sat together at the end of the hall, and looked out of windows that displayed a beautiful ocean and sunsets.

I would meet with them individually each day. But all they wanted to talk about was each other. They were deliriously happy, and each felt deeply for the other, which included a strong spiritual connection. They could each sense what the other was thinking, feeling, and hoping. Talking was often unnecessary because they could both sense what the other would say. They would tell me this consistently, and I would validate it with the other. It was a form of love one rarely sees.

Carolyn's parents were struggling with this relationship. They wanted Carolyn to be happy in the midst of the peril she was facing. But they also didn't want her to possibly endure the feelings that might come should the relationship come to an end. They wanted to protect her from the pain and emotional upheaval a love relationship can sometimes bring. They knew this would only weaken her even more.

In a special session with Carolyn and her parents, she explained what would eventually help both of them to be put at ease. Carolyn said, *"I never thought I would ever know love as you two know love. But Alan has given me a chance to get just a sense of what it must be like to love someone so deeply. We will never make love. We will never have a wedding, and, Daddy, I have dreams of you walking me down the aisle. Alan and I will never be able to have children or give you grandchildren. But our love for one another is so genuine, so sincere, we truly believe God is with us and for us. Mom, Dad, we want your blessing. We want you to share in our joy."*

Alan would bring his own understanding of the relationship. He would, in a counseling session, say, *"I don't know what to do! I didn't ever expect to fall in love with someone. I don't know how this happened. For so long, I would wake up, and the first thing I would think about is that I have cancer and it's killing me. The last thing I would think about before I went to sleep at night is that I have cancer and it's killing me. But now, Carolyn is the first and last thing I think about every day. I want so much to live as long as I possibly can because I don't want to lose even one moment of life with her. I know many will judge us and consider our relationship to be nothing more than a distraction from our fight with cancer. I also know we will never be able to experience what it means to be a couple. But I do know that I truly love Carolyn and she truly loves me. We both believe there will be a life eternal and we will be together."*

Carolyn and Alan would eventually be discharged from the hospital but would remain at the clinic for further treatment. They saw each other every day, but they had agreed to be sure that Carolyn's family and friends would also be given time to be together. Eventually, I was able to bring them all in for counseling, and it wasn't long before the four of them were regularly together. Alan had no family, but Carolyn's parents began to realize they had anough room in their lives to "adopt" Alan into the family, and Alan accepted.

I continued to provide them counseling, but the cancer was winning. Both were so weak they were readmitted to the hospital and placed in a special wing of the facility that I had been asked to create: seven beds dedicated to those who would die. Every staff member had been given special training, including the woman who emptied the trash. Everyone on this wing had volunteered to be a part of an experiment to create an environment to support patients and their families at a very dramatic moment—the time of death. In fact, it came to be known, unofficially, as the death ward.

Carolyn was admitted first, but Alan was admitted two days later. I asked they be placed in adjacent rooms. They wanted to be in the same room, but hospital protocol would not permit it. Both were so weak they couldn't get out of bed, and both were on oxygen support. Carolyn's family and Alan had agreed to no longer fight the cancer. They had elected to only receive pain medication. Water and glycerin swabs were the only things they were being given. They became the talk of the hospital. Two lovers, coming to the end of life. Each thinking only of the welfare of the other.

"Is Alan taking his pain medication? Is he still able to take it in a cocktail? Tell him I'm not going to be awake much longer. I'm so tired, and my time is soon. I sense it's soon for him too. Please, go be with him, Dr. Stephenson. I don't want him to die alone, and he has no one else but us and you. Tell him I will be waiting for him on the other side."

I went next door and found Alan barely able to talk. *"I'm on my way. I don't even feel like I'm here anymore. Tell C I will be waiting for her with open arms on the other side. Go. I want to be alone. I want to be with C."*

I went back to Carolyn's room, and her parents were in tears. Carolyn had just died. I stayed with them for a while and then went back to Alan's room. The nurses were all around him. The doctor had just pronounced Alan's time of death.

I remain convinced Alan and Carolyn were close and together in life, in death, and in life after death. I even think they planned the end. They were so in tune with each other they knew how to go out together. I was able to witness two people who were deeply in love but unable to truly express it because of her age and because of their health. Yet they would capture the imagination of those around them. It was truly a love story unspoken.

Gratitude

When it seems
all before me is dark,
I need to remember
so it seemed to many
who have gone on before me.
When mistrust and doubt are upon me;
and I am battling despair,
I need to remember
the great and good
of every time
have had to find their way,
as I must,
by their courage
and in confidence and trust.
I need to remember to keep close company
with their spirits.

This poem is dedicated to all my clients who entrusted me to be with them and counsel them in the last days of their lives.

William Stephenson, PhD

And So It Goes

It was late, and the storm was relentless, even for the Pacific Northwest. As I turned in to go to bed, I was thinking of how relieved I felt that I didn't have to be anywhere that night. Just as I crawled into bed, I heard someone pounding on my front door and the person seemed to be calling out my name. I was alone in my Seattle home, and all the lights were out.

I got up, put on my bathrobe, and went to the door. I turned on the porch light and yelled through the front door, *"Who is it? Who's out there?"*

A moaning, sobbing voice responded as the person continued pounding on the door. *"Please, please let me in. I can't live like this any longer! Please!"*

I opened the door and in stumbled this elderly woman, soaked from the rain. Her hair was disheveled and dripping from the storm. She was shivering from the cold, wet, sobbing through it all and unable to make any sense of her situation.

I turned on the heat, lit a fire, and started the coffee. I sensed that this was going to be a long night. Then I suggested she go in and shower and get some dry clothes I had selected I thought she could wear.

I said, *"Mrs. Truxton, I insist that you do these few things or I won't be able to help you. But if you shower and change, this will give you a few moments to breathe and calm yourself so that we can talk this through. Otherwise, I need to call 911."*

Thirty minutes later, she came back into the living room, sat down, and just stared at the floor. There was little improvement of her state of mind. *"Why did you come here, Mrs. Truxton, and how did you find me?"*

She said, *"I heard you give a lecture about your work with the terminally ill. And, you're in the phone book. Dr. Stephenson, I need your help. Ever since my husband died, I haven't been able to function. I can't live like this any longer. You've got to take my case. You've got to!"*

I never see clients in my home and rarely see adults without children in a life-threatening crisis, but saying no to someone in distress at midnight didn't seem like a good idea. *"Mrs. Truxton, tell me your story."*

"Just before my husband died, we had a terrible argument. Before we went to bed, I screamed at him, 'I wish you were dead!' The next morning, I woke up and next to me was my dead husband."

She said, "I am responsible for my husband's death. It's my fault. I have been burdened by this guilt. I was too distraught to go to the funeral. I often never get out of bed. I don't know how to live alone. I cry constantly. I rarely venture out of the house. I've stopped seeing my friends or going to my church because I just keep crying. Even my children have grown weary of me, and they don't want the grandchildren around me. My world has come to an end, and all I want to do is die."

As the hour of counseling came to a close, I decided to extend it to two. Both of us exhausted, we set up a schedule of times we would meet, including the next day. I asked her if she thought she could drive home, and she reassured me that she was very capable. The storm outside and the storm inside seemed to be abating.

"Mrs. Truxton, do you have feelings of wanting to kill yourself?"

"Not anymore, Dr. Stephenson. I feel like I have some hope that I haven't had for a long time."

Just as she was leaving, I asked her, "By the way, Mrs. Truxton, I meant to ask you, how long ago did your husband die?"

She said, "It's been eleven years ago yesterday. And it seems like it was only yesterday."

It would take several months of therapy and medication management to resolve the issues in her life. Grief is a strange animal, and time doesn't heal all wounds. In fact, for Mrs. Truxton, her watch had stopped.

Fishing With Bread

Our cruise ship ported at Mykonos, a small island off the coast of Greece, for an overnight stay. Early the next morning, before sunrise, I went for a walk along the pier. All was quiet, and as the sun began to rise, I could see a man fishing about a quarter of a mile down from the ship. As I came up to him, I was to meet an old man, chain-smoking and fishing with gear that might have been on display in an antique shop.

I introduced myself, and he spoke very little English. But he was willing to stumble through the limits of our separate languages, and we got to know each other. I eventually asked him if I could borrow his fishing pole and fish for a half hour. He smiled and said he'd be honored. He reeled in his line, and there were over a dozen small hooks attached to the line, all empty of bait. I asked, *"What do you use for bait?"*

"Bread! Of course!"

"How do you keep the bread on the hook once it gets in the water?"

He smiled and said, *"I show you."* And he went into his old beat-up car and pulled out a piece of very stale, very hard bread. He looked at me and instructed: *"You bite into bread and then put on hook! No?"*

We both smiled, and we both bit into this very hard loaf of bread. Two old men, one from a wealthy and powerful nation, and the other, toothless and weather-worn from an island I could barely pronounce. Neither one of us could speak the other's language, but it didn't matter.

We took the chewed bread out of our mouths, and together we attached it to the hooks and began to giggle like two kids playing hooky with a fishing pole. We cast the line into the water, continued to chew on this very hard bread, and waited in silence.

I suddenly realized I was on holy ground. Two old men, from very different countries far apart, coming together and discovering we both had the same address. We both realized we belonged to the same family. We were brothers forever after this fishing tale would come to an end.

Whenever I feel like I've forgotten where I live, and I do often when senseless violence is committed . . . Dallas, Orlando, Minneapolis, Baton Rouge, Las Vegas . . . I forget sometimes where I am living. That is when I close my eyes and remember a toothless old man with a cigarette dangling from his mouth, helping me bait a hook. Then I remember my address: The human family. The Mind of God.

Living In A Waiting Room

A task we must all learn
If we are going to find
Wholeness and wellness,
Is to learn to live in a waiting room.

We are often confronted with waiting.
Waiting for the lab report after that biopsy.
Waiting for the surgeon to come and tell you the news.
Waiting for that long distance call from some distant hospital
Where the life of someone you care about is hanging in the balance.
Waiting for that call from your son or daughter driving a long distance.
Waiting for healing to come in a broken relationship and discovering
That forgiveness and reconciliation can't be forced.
Waiting for that family misunderstanding to get better.
Waiting for that loss to not hurt as bad as it does now.
Waiting with that loneliness that no relationship you have can alleviate.

Learning to live in a waiting room
Is a vital discipline
To recovery
To wellness.
It's our opportunity to evaluate what we're going after
And whether what we are waiting for is worth the wait.

Learning to live in a waiting room is a gift of God.
A time to discipline yourself.
To see if what we are waiting for is really worth it.

William Stephenson, PhD

The Art of Waiting

Life is filled with waiting, and sometimes it's as if the world is one large waiting room. Some people feel like that character in William Saroyan's play, *The Time of Your Life*, who says, "The more you wait, the less there is to wait for." A lot of people grow tired of waiting. They get impatient, and they quit. Waiting is such an important part of our lives. It is crucial to learn how to wait creatively, expectantly, and hopefully.

I was asked to counsel a family whose newborn son was born with his brain outside of his skull. He lived for seventeen days. His entire family—mother, father, grandparents, aunts, uncles, cousins—all surrounded this baby with love. But to care for this newborn, and each other, they had to learn to wait lovingly, effectively, creatively, unselfishly. Otherwise, in time, the tension and anxiety would become so great that waiting for the baby to die could begin to destroy one another. There is a kind of waiting that is destructive.

A married couple came for counseling. They were so close on many things. However, she had a deeply religious experience that changed her life. She wanted her husband to share it with her. But her waiting for him to share in this religious lifestyle was done arrogantly and smugly. Her religious experience would eventually drive them apart even with the counseling. She knew how to believe, but she didn't know how to wait. She wouldn't learn how to wait creatively and lovingly.

One young woman was twenty-one years old. She went through a passage of rebellion in which she did some things that were unthinkable by most people. Her parents judged she was permanently lost to the street. They told her they could not tolerate her behavior any longer. Telling her this broke their relationship. This young lady, with professional care, was able to get through that passage, but not with them, without them. Despite attempts to bring them together, no words were exchanged. The parents didn't know how to wait, creatively, lovingly.

It's the quality of waiting that makes the difference whether or not a relationship will survive. That quality comes when we are able to alter our expectations about the future because that is what brings power into the present.

William Stephenson, PhD

Listening To My Heart

I fish. There's something about fishing that gives me calm and connection. I fish on a pier in San Diego that spans more than six hundred feet out over the Pacific Ocean. On any given day, there will be more than thirty others who will be throwing their line over the side. We get to know each other, those of us who are "regulars." But mixed into our lot will be some people who are homeless, the resident walkers and many tourists will take the long walk out to the end of the pier.

In the middle of the pier is a café with fantastic breakfast burritos. I fish here because I also get to observe people, all coming with different agendas. It's also a place where some will come and walk to the end but not come back. The rip tide is so severe at the end of the pier that if you jump off from there you won't come back to the surface. This is the story of one of them. Her name was Amy.

Early one morning, I was standing at the entrance to the pier, talking with some fellow fishermen and we were all about to walk out further along the pier to our favorite places to fish. But I noticed a well-dressed young lady about to go on the pier. Too well dressed for such an occasion as not to be noticed.

As she was about to pass me, I said, *"Good morning. How's it going for you today?"*

She stopped and looked at me for what seemed a very long moment and then she said something with no emotion at all: *"I'm going to walk to the end of the pier, but I'm not coming back."*

I immediately knew that my fishing for that day was not going to happen. I walked closer to her so that I could talk to her in a calm voice. *"As you are walking on the pier, may I walk with you? There's a café in the middle of the pier and they make great coffee. Can I buy you a cup? And as we walk, would you tell me about yourself? My name is Bill and I'm a counseling psychologist. I sense that you are in a lot of hurt right now and I want you to tell me about it."*

"My name is Amy and I'm from Phoenix. I came up here because I was promised a job and some girls I had known in college said that I could live with them and share the apartment. But when I got here there was no job *and these girls had given the space in the apartment to someone else and then someone broke into my car and stole all my stuff, including my phone and computer. I am so devastated that all I want to do is die and that's why I'm here and that's what I'm going to go and do!*

We continued to walk together in silence and as we neared the café I said to Amy, "Your day is worse than you thought. Not only did you not get the job, or have a place to live, but you're also not going to jump off this pier. Today you will not kill yourself."

She remained unresponsive. I got her a cup of coffee and we continued our walk to the end of the pier as the sun began to peek over the horizon. We stopped to look at the sun rise, overlooking the eastern rails of the pier. In the water were dozens of surfers and on the pier were the many fishermen throwing their lines into the sea.

"Amy, do you see all these people in and around this pier? This is their pier. It's a very important part of their life. How do you think they will feel if you tried to kill yourself from their pier?"

"I don't think they would care. They don't know me. Why should they care?"

"They may not know you personally. But to watch another human being suddenly die is going to have a major emotional effect on them. Many will wish they hadn't been here today. Some may not want to come back. Others will grieve because they witnessed your death. No, Amy, your death will have quite an impact upon them. Not to mention your family and friends. Can you imagine how they will feel? How do I tell your parents?"

With tears in her eyes, she spoke trying to catch her breath at the same time, "I just don't know what to do, where to go, who to turn to! I feel so alone!"

"Amy, I want you to do something for me. Actually, I want you to do something for yourself. Right now, you're thinking and making decisions from out of your head. Take a moment and just breathe. And then, I want you to ask yourself, 'What does my heart say about all this? What is my heart saying to me right now?'"

She took a moment and then she fell into my arms and just sobbed. Several minutes later I escorted her to the café to use the bathroom and sit and continue our conversation.

"I'm not going to hurt myself any longer, Dr. Stephenson."

"Amy, I prepared for you what I call a safe contract. If you begin to feel suicidal, I want you to look at this and remember you telling me that you were safe and wouldn't self-harm. And here is a list of places to help you get home. Here is my phone and I want you to call someone back home to tell them you are on your way back."

She did as I asked and then signed the "safe contract" as I had. I walked her to the entrance way to the pier, gave her a hug and wished her well. She also had my card and knew she could call anytime.

As she neared her car, she turned to me, placed her hand over her heart and mouthed so I could understand, *"I'm listening to my heart."* She turned, got in her car and drove away.

She would become the fourth person I would stop from suiciding off the Ocean Beach Pier.

Amy had come to believe that "ending it all" would be doing everyone else a favor and, she would no longer have to face the grim struggle of beginning again. But she was able to let go of all the failures she had recently endured and, with just a readjustment of her "framework" she was able to choose to create a new beginning.

William Stephenson, PhD

Our Lonely Self

When we listen to our loneliness
We discover that learning
How to live with others
Is secondary to learning
How to live with ourselves.

It is in the wilderness
Of our loneliness
That we learn to find
Our Center.

It is in the wilderness
Of our loneliness
That we learn to better care
For others.

It is in the wilderness
Of our loneliness
Where we learn
To feel more compassion
For others,

It is only when we go
Deeper into ourselves
That we learn to go further
With others.

That is God's sense of humor.
An irony, at least.
God so made us,
That only as we are able
To withdraw and be alone
Are we better prepared
To live with others.

William Stephenson, PhD

A Room Without a View

I have a room
I go to on occasion.
It's dark, foreboding, cold, and damp.
It's called the room of remorse.

This is a room
I go into whenever I get depressed.
I crawl inside this room and I begin
to think of all my mistakes,
all my regrets.

In this room,
I grieve over all the things
I wished I hadn't done
the things I should have done
and didn't do.

This is the room
where I can breathe my mistakes,
where I can re-live my shame,
where I can ponder my ugliness.

From this room
I yearn to be released
To be free to know that life can begin again.
To be free of the prison of the past.
To dwell in the room of forgiveness.

William Stephenson, PhD

A Dead Stump

There was that day
When we watched the nurse
Pull the sheet over the tired face
Of someone we thought
Would never die.

There was that day
When we stood ankle deep
In the broken pieces of a
Ruined relationship we pledged
Would never end.

There was that day
When ugly circumstances,
Not of our own choosing
Came raining roughshod
Down upon us.

William Stephenson, PhD

These are the times
When we feel our lives are
Like a dead stump.
As if life has ended.

That is when we need to hear
The whisper from someone who says,
"Life can begin again."

In The Heart

A poem
I've come to believe begins,
"There is no end of things in the heart."[1]

If
I take something to heart
It will always be there for me.
No matter what happens
It will always be there for me,
Waiting.

Whether it's a person,
A place,
A dream,
A relationship.
Something sacred.

It is all part of the same
And will always be there
Carrying the same beat
As my heart.

At night
When I try to sleep
But cannot,
That is when all of the pathways
Seem to connect
And I see the people
I have loved and helped and hurt.

William Stephenson, PhD

I see
Their hands reach for me.
I hear the beat and see
And understand
What they all mean to me.

It is
In those quiet moments
That I know there is no end of
Things in the heart.

The Pure in Heart

What does it mean to be a purist?
Have you ever known one?
Have you ever worked with one?
Have you ever lived with one?

The people who think they are purists
Are convinced that there's
Only one right way to the truth.
Only one right way to approach a problem.
Only one right way of dealing with something.
Only one right answer,
And they have it.

To have a purist in your life
Is to be content to be a follower.
You can never be an equal.

The surest way
To destroy a friendship
To wreck a marriage
To alienate a child or parent
To ruin a relationship
Is to desire purity.

The best way
To wreck a child's self esteem
Is to instill in them this goal
Of having to
Be pure.
No mistakes.

Purity
Is really a paradox.
The most spiritually mature people
Are seldom aware
Of their own goodness.

Purity
Needs to be clarified.
True purists are blessed
When they are not driven
By mixed motives, for
They will see God.

They will see what is permanent.
They will see what will last.
They will see what is truly sacred.

To be a true purist
Is to be sacred.
To be in relationships
That are caring
And loving
And nurturing.

To see what is essential.
Which is to see persons as sacred
In our homes and in the greater community.
To see the best in others and for others.
To declare that we are each a child of God.

It is then
That we understand the Beatitude…
"Blessed are the pure in heart,
For they will see God
With a liberated heart."

To Be A Child Again

Because of
A garden I have helped design
And the fish I always seek
And the birds that fill my quiet morning time...

Because of
My family's love
And my enemy's family...

Because of
The hope of the homeless
And the hunger of the hopeless...

Because of
My need of community bread
And love from a woman with faith...

On this other side of a half-lived life
I yearn to be like a little child again.
To be held against the breast of God
Who quiets my fears,
Who encourages my faith to begin again...
And again.

William Stephenson, PhD

As a child again
I can embrace
This great and gracious Mystery
Who parents me through
This mysterious plan of my life
Who created me in His image
Revealed His likeness,
My likeness...

On this day of gratitude
I ask for the wild courage
To be a child of God again
And seek to become
What I have now dared to claim.

Christal With an "I"

She was just twelve years old. Her name was Christal. I kept using a "y" but she insisted on the "i." I used to tease her about that. It was our way of finding something to smile about. She would then tell me my name should be a "v" instead of a "ph." But I insisted on the "ph." And then we would start thinking of other names we could play this game with.

She was dying. I would be the family therapist for the six short weeks I came to know them. Christal had cystic fibrosis, some retardation, and had battled pneumonia on a regular basis. It would kill her eventually.

Christal came from a very poor family. They couldn't afford the expensive medical care she needed, including a therapist. I'm not cheap, but sometimes I am free. Her family ended up declaring bankruptcy and sold their house. All to give Christal the care they wanted for their daughter.

They are amazing parents.

Christal's main issue was she knew she would never make it to thirteen; to be a teenager. She wanted the symbol a teen represented versus what a child represented. She was grieving over what could not be, not what she was dealing with physically.

Christal was also feeling guilty because she knew the financial bind the family was in because of her illness. She worried that her parents would not be able to afford new oxygen tanks or the breathing medicine.

One night, she asked me to come and sit with her because she was unable to get to sleep and she was afraid she couldn't breathe if she fell asleep, even though she was on oxygen 24/7. In the dark, I sat and together we breathed.

I asked her, *"Christal, when you are in bed alone at night, how do you slow your breathing so you can go to sleep?"*

She said, *"I look out my window at all of the stars. I then start naming them after all the people who have helped me and have loved me. But I always run out of stars."* And, we began to name the stars that night until she fell asleep.

When there is so little time, I become deeply attached to my clients and their family. Christal was no exception. I would see her and her parents nearly every day. There were good days and scary days. She was in and out of the hospital on a regular basis, trying to manage her bouts with pneumonia. I had to go away for eight days. It had been planned before I came to know her, and she knew I was going to be gone. She encouraged me to go because she knew I needed some time with my family; she valued family very much. She said she would still be here when I got back. But while I was gone, I checked in daily: her status was worsening. She was in hospice care, and they thought it would be very soon.

I returned and immediately went to her bedside. I said, *"Hi, Christal with a 'y.'"*

She said, *"Hi, Dr. Stephenson with a 'v.'"* I sat, and we just looked at each other. Every breath was so painful for her. She said from behind her oxygen mask, *"I waited for you."*

Tears in my eyes, I said, *"I love you, Christal with an 'i.'"* *"I love you, Dr. Stephenson with a 'ph.'"*

She would die late that night with parents, grandparents, and myself in the background. Early the next morning, as her parents and I were having coffee together in the hospital cafe, they said, *"Dr. Stephenson, we have decided to take all of the memorial money and give it to the Cystic Fibrosis Foundation, and we also plan to be speakers to support this cause. We want other parents to know they are not alone."*

I smiled and knew they didn't need me any longer. They were on their way. They were broke and deeply in debt, and yet they were full of hope. No, they didn't need me anymore. My work was done.

Choices I

We are free
To choose our reaction
To all that happens to us.

We are free
To determine
Whether that reaction will lead
To life or lead to death.

We are free
To choose what will become
A blessing and what will be a curse.

We are free
To choose how we handle
Even the worst of tragedy.

William Stephenson, PhD

And they come to me
To talk about their choices - -
"I can't live with myself any longer!"
"How can I ever forgive myself?"
"I can't stand the pain I'm causing to others."
"I'm better off dead than alive."

What should I say to their choices?
To their consequences?
To their decisions?

Do I say?
"Well, that's too bad.
Other people have done worse things."
That will not bring peace.

Do I say?
"From now on, you will punish yourself,
And maybe,
Just maybe,
You will be able to punish yourself enough so that
Just before you die
You will find peace."

No one could ever do enough, I fear.

Or, do I say:
"There is in our souls
A grace that falls on each of us.
We look to the One who showed us
Just how far that grace will go for us.
Take that grace and embrace it by
Being gracious to those around you.
It's your choice."

What Are You In For?

I am convinced that the cruelest form of punishment is having to eat alone. We often use it with those who can no longer independently participate in the community such as a church or synagogue.

"*What did you do wrong?*"

"*Arthritis and a broken hip. I'm unable to get out of the house.*"

"*Yeah, that'll do it.*"

"*And you, what did you do?*"

"*My husband died, and I'm eighty-six.*"

"*Aha! That serves you right!*"

Two stories.

I was asked to provide counseling to two women who were both diagnosed as being terminally ill. Both women were widows, and both of them lived alone. These women taught me to understand the power of inclusiveness.

Mrs. Henderson. Terminally ill and living in a skilled nursing facility. Beautiful place. Lots of visitor parking spaces, but not one car using them. I found her room, and the staff eventually wheeled her into the area I was to use to conduct the interview.

The first thing I said was, "*What are you in for?*"

She said, "*Talking to myself.*"

"*Ah! That'll do it.*"

Apparently, she belonged to a large church with several ministers, choirs, fellowship groups, and several women's groups, Bible classes, and groups that take trips.

"*How long has it been since anybody from your church came to visit, Mrs. Henderson?*"

"*You're the first person to come visit me since my husband's funeral in over three months, and you're not even from the church.*"

Punishment for getting sick and talking to herself. Make her eat alone.

Another client, Mrs. Rollins. A woman in her mid-seventies, living in a beautiful home overlooking the Los Angeles basin. She now lived alone since her husband had died. On the mantel were pictures of all her kids and grandchildren who apparently lived on the East Coast. All too busy to come and visit.

She said, *"Sit down and relax. I'll go and fix us some lunch. It won't take long."*

I hadn't planned on eating. But after several minutes, I got restless sitting there all alone, so I went looking for her. She had a large formal dining room that could seat over a dozen at the table, which was beautifully adorned with the finest of china and linens with creases two inches deep.

I said, *"Mrs. Rollins, we could have just as easily eaten in the kitchen."* But she kept at it. Cloth napkins in silver rings. Stemmed crystal ware. Beautiful silverware. Candles in silver candlesticks.

"Mrs. Rollins, there's no need for all this formality."

"Dr. Stephenson, my doctor told me why you're here. Will you please be quiet and sit down?"

"Yes, ma'am, I was going to do that next."

She said, *"Apparently, you don't know what it's like to fix a meal for one."*

"No, ma'am, I don't."

She and I sat at her beautiful dining room table together, and we had a banquet. There were many of us that day. She assured me that the number around the table that day was twice as many as she had had in months and months and months.

I would be going to see both women on a regular basis, but always when it was time to eat. It would not be long before their cancer became so overwhelming that they could not host or eat with me. But there were stories. They kept repeating the times we sat and ate together.

On Holy Ground

I was visiting a client who was in the hospital to undergo an experimental treatment for her advanced form of cancer. We had become good friends, and toward the end of our session we were laughing and having a good time.

Evidently, a patient in the adjoining room had overheard our conversation about how to live until we die, and she asked the nurse if I would come and visit her after I was finished with my client.

I want to pause and paint a picture of the patient I walked in to meet. Day and night she had to have an oxygen tube in her nostrils in order to stay alive. The cancer was in both lungs, and she was slowly suffocating to death. The cancer was also in her bones and joints and back, and she was in constant pain, even though she was heavily medicated. Every movement was agony for her.

This lady would die in this tiny room, alone. Seldom, if ever, did anyone ever come to visit or offer her a word of comfort. She said, *"They don't know what to say, and they can't bear watching me in such pain."*

This woman's mind, however, was as sharp as any mind I knew. This woman's spirit was more lovely than any flower arrangement or any symphony of an orchestra. I sensed that I was in the presence of a teacher and my soul was about to be enriched.

I sat down with her, and we talked. She said, *"I need to talk to someone who will listen, and I believe you are the one to do that."*

"Yes, ma'am. I will listen, but from time to time, I want to tell you what I hear you saying. Deal?"

"Deal."

For over an hour, this woman would talk about her life, her family, and her faith. She told me what she was proud of and what she was ashamed of. At the end of the hour, we were both exhausted.

As I prepared to leave, I said, *"Mamie, before I go, can I tell you a joke?"*

Her eyes lit up, and I told her a joke. It was funny. I'm not going to tell you the joke, but it was very funny.

And then she said, *"Dr. Stephenson, can I tell you a joke?"*

She told me one, and it too was very funny. We both laughed. There was a moment when I felt as if my soul was at one with her soul. There, in that room of death, a seasoned psychotherapist and a cancer-stricken lady, both of us surrounded by the smells of disinfectant and death, giggling like two kids caught with their hands in the cookie jar!

When we finished laughing, we paused and just looked at each other in silence for several moments. I leaned over and gave her a kiss on her cheek, and then she kissed me. It was a sacred moment. I felt like I wanted to take off my shoes because I knew I was standing on holy ground. We were never to see each other again.

I Was Wrong

I have spent a lifetime
trying to find meaning in my life.

I thought my work
would give meaning to my life.

I thought providing counseling to people in distress
would give me meaning.

I was wrong.

The meaning isn't in the work
if it isn't, first of all, in the person.

I thought by seeking happiness,
I would find meaning in my life.

I was wrong.

Happiness can't be forced.
It's always a by-product.

I thought I could get meaning for my life
by getting it from my significant relationships.

I was wrong.

If I don't take meaning into a relationship,
I will never get any meaning out of it.

I thought God
had the meaning for my life.

I was wrong.

William Stephenson, PhD

God gives me life,
not meaning.

What I give back to God in my life
is the meaning I seek.

Sanity Is Where You Find It

We often try to explain the unexplainable by declaring "temporary insanity." For example, a young husband came home and the kids were jumping on the couch, the house was a mess, the dog had chased the cat up the drapes and he hears his wife humming in the locked bathroom where she was taking a leisurely bath. He knocked on the door and yelled, *"Why are you in there and they're out here?"* And she said, *"They were driving me up the wall and if I didn't take some quiet time I would have gone crazy!"* "Sanity," said Will Rogers, *"is where you find it."*

A young mother who was once my client, would once a week or so go out in the garage, sit in the car, roll up the windows and scream for five minutes at the top of her lungs! Then she went back into the house and lived another week with a family, which, she was told, was a gift of God. Sanity is where you find it.

The probation department sent a man to me for counseling who was going to the unemployment office every day, looking for work, and had been arrested for throwing a lemon meringue pie in the face of the woman behind the counter. When asked why he did it, he said, *"Every day of the week, I've been standing in that long line and when I'd get up to the counter, she'd say, with that bureaucratic smile, 'There's no job today.'"*

He said, *"One day I just snapped! I went to a nearby bakery, bought a lemon meringue pie, came back and threw it in her face!"* Knowing that they knew who he was, he went to a nearby police station and turned himself in. *"But,"* he said, *"I felt better."* Indeed. Sanity is where you find it.

William Stephenson, PhD

A Recurring Nightmare

Monica was just twenty-seven. She was single. She called herself a born-again Christian. She had no family that came to visit her as I recall. She was dying of cancer. She asked for me.

I would come to her bedside, and we would talk. Well, she did the talking. She talked incessantly. She talked about her childhood and adolescence. She talked about both of her marriages. She talked about her two miscarriages and one abortion. She owned a lot of unresolved grief and a load of guilt that clashed with her beliefs.

But throughout all her conversations she kept reminding me, or herself, how she had come to know Jesus and the conversional moment when she accepted Christ into her life. It was just after she had been diagnosed with fourth stage lymphocytic leukemia.

She shared with me the extensive and painful treatment she had undergone. She said, *"My fellow church members had been so supportive in the beginning, but now that I have been diagnosed as terminal, they seemed less so."* She said, *"They don't know what to say, so they stay away."*

She was not the same Monica they had known. She now had no hair, was emaciated and in constant need of transfusions. There would be no remission for her. She said when people looked at her she could see their fear. Her visitor's registration book was nearly empty.

She seemed dismayed, unsure, anxious. I continued to counsel her on her current state, and I remained committed to assisting her in staying in the moment, staying in the present, knowing her death was imminent.

She continued each session with her confidence in Jesus, believing he would save her so she could go on missionary trips around the world. She said, *"I am determined that if I get out of the hospital, I will dedicate the rest of my life to service for others."*

She continued to be in terrible pain, but she refused all pain medications. The pain medications could manage the pain without rendering her unconscious, but she felt the need to stay alert and wait for one more round of chemotherapy that would save her life. But there would not be one more round.

Late one weekend afternoon, when many of the patients in the hospice were out visiting family or going for a walk, Monica used that time to talk to the staff about her faith and how she was ready, as she said, *"to go be with Jesus."* Her ability to thrive was declining rapidly, and early that same evening, she collapsed.

She was put in her bed, and the hospice team did everything they could to make her comfortable. She was close to death, but she asked I come to her bedside as soon as possible. When I arrived, she began to cry. It was a frightened cry, like a small child who was lost with no one to help her.

"Dr. Stephenson, is it time for me to die? I'm not ready yet. I'm not ready yet. I don't want to die. I don't want to die! Please. Hold me. I'm so scared!"

I reached down and took her in my arms and held her, but she continued to cry, and her distress now became known by everyone around us. It was as if no one could understand what needed to be done. Monica suddenly hemorrhaged. She began to expel blood from her mouth, nose, and rectum.

I continued to hold her as she kept pleading, *"I don't want to die! I don't want—"* Then, she lost consciousness, and died soon after.

I don't remember much of what transpired after that. Nurses said I was covered in blood. They tried to speak to me, but they could tell I was not able to hear them. They said I was unable to speak or respond to any voice for nearly three days. Weeks went by, and I had night terrors that disrupted my household. I wasn't fit to see clients, I was scaring my own children, I lost weight.

Therapy, especially group therapy, helped me get past what I judged to be my biggest failure. I would have other "failures" that would challenge my commitment to this work I had chosen for myself, but Monica's death reminded me of ghosts that would haunt me and wake me up in a cold sweat on occasion.

Where Do I Go?

As I sit here in the cold, dampness
   that is in my life, I realize
   I have lost the joy
   I had in my life
   I once had inside me . . .
   The hope I had in tomorrow . . .

Gone.

I am so completely alone.

I need my soul to kiss me again,
   to touch me with tenderness
   warm and wet upon my skin
   and whisper in my heart
   the claim upon me,
   the claim life has upon me.

In my wider world . . .
   so dark and weary . . .
   a mystery without an answer . . .
   my thoughts reach out
   with trembling fingers into the
   vastness before me,
   grasping at life's larger meaning.

The faces of those who wait for me
   overwhelm my capacity to give what they need,
   and I am lost in their pleas.

O soul,
   if I could just learn
   to kiss the joy
   as it flies, as it flies . . .

(Author's note: This poem's title and content came from a sixteen-year-old who was in an advanced stage of cancer with parents constantly fighting.)

Panic

Panic
May be the ultimate enemy
Of the human spirit.

Panic
Can play havoc with your head,
Causing you to want
To throw in the towel.
At the very time you need to stand firm.

Panic
Causes you to make a lot of stupid,
Self-defeating mistakes
At the very time you need clear-thinking.

It can cause you to
Resign,
Run,
Retreat
At the very time you need to be
Resolute.

Panic
Can make you feel
As if you are running madly
In all directions
At the very time
When you need energy
To pull things together.

Panic
Is indeed the enemy
Of the human spirit.

William Stephenson, PhD

Panic And A Peaceful Heart

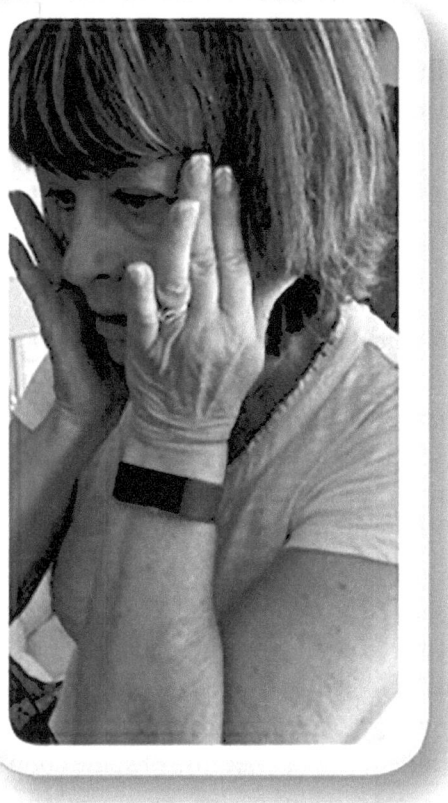

"I was so ashamed, I could just die." That is what he said, and then he did. They don't know whether he died because he was ashamed for lying or because he was caught in a lie. But the last thing he said was, *"I'm so ashamed, I could die."* And he did. Then his wife, hours later, also died.

This story is not some television reality show episode. It's a story found in the Bible in the Book of Acts. Two people who went into a panic collapsed and died when faced with the painful truth. As physicians well know, the body has a way of acting out what the mind believes.

Dr. George Engel, in an article published in the *Annals of Internal Medicine*, entitled, "Sudden and Rapid Death during Psychological Stress," reports the results of a study of persons who died after receiving some distressing news.

The greatest single category of sudden death from stress or emotional shock were those who had been suddenly confronted with some grave personal danger. The second largest category of sudden death due to stress were those who had heard of the death or serious injury of a loved one. The third greatest category of those who died of sudden death due to emotional shock, Dr. Engel found, were those who suffered from some severe humiliation and recognition that their personal status had been wounded. Interestingly enough, more men than women died in that category of severe humiliation and battered egos.

I had a client who was discouraged and depressed and saw himself as a failure. Doctors said there was nothing physically wrong with him, but in spite of what the doctors said, he lost his will to live, his heart got the message, and it obeyed.

Dr. Engel's study affirms that our minds are miraculous, and they have a great deal of power over the behavior of our bodies. Which begs the question: Is panic contagious? Can we catch it from each other?

The *Los Angeles Times* reported an event that happened at a high school football game in nearby Monterey Park. Four spectators, during a game, came and reported they were nauseous and vomiting and felt faint. A quick conclusion was made that there was food poisoning from an orange drink at the snack bar because of some copper wiring. Because the loudspeakers weren't working, they instructed the cheerleaders to go in front of the bleachers and tell the crowd not to drink the orange drink because food poisoning was suspected.

Within minutes, nearly two hundred people reported being nauseous and began to vomit and faint. By ambulances and private cars, they were all rushed to emergency rooms at nearby hospitals.

But it was a false alarm. While the doctors all found them suffering from symptoms of food poisoning, when they were analyzed, none of the food or drink in that snack bar was contaminated. When the people were told that, their symptoms left them as quickly as they had come.

Behavior is contagious. What we put into our minds affects our bodies, and if I may use computerese: "Garbage in, garbage out. What we put into our minds matters a great deal.

The late Dr. Norman Cousins, in his book *The Healing Heart*, tells of an experience he had on a golf course. He noticed an ambulance and paramedics working on a man lying on a stretcher. Because Cousins himself was a survivor of a massive heart attack, he rushed over and noticed that the paramedics were doing what they were trained to do. Everyone was watching the gauges and monitors they had hooked up to the man. But no one was looking at the man.

Cousins looked at the man's face and saw his panic and then saw that the cardiac monitor indicated that his heartbeat was so rapid that he was about to go into shock, and so he went over and put his hand on the man and said, *"You've got a fine heart."*

The man said, *"How do you know?"*

"I can see it on the cardiograph. And, furthermore, you're about to be taken to one of the finest hospitals in the country and you're going to be just fine."

The man's panic began to subside because something else was going into his mind, and he began to look around and became interested and involved in what was happening. Dr. Cousins went on to say to him, *"It's a hot day, and you're dehydrated, and that effects the electrical shocks in your heart, and you're going to be all right."* And he was.

What we put into our minds has a great deal to do with whether panic will dwell in our hearts. Garbage in, garbage out.

Francis MacNutt, a pioneer in the limitless possibilities of the human spirit, tells a story his mother told about him when he was a little boy. He was being punished by his mother, and she said, *"Francis, you have to go and stand in that corner."* In recalling that incident, his mother said that Francis replied to her, *"Mother, I refuse to regard this as a corner!"* You can't worry about a boy like that.

But that's what we need to tell ourselves when we are in a crisis. I remind my clients that they have options. They get to select their emotions and their reactions to stressful events. They may not be able to change those circumstances, but they can choose their attitude toward those circumstances and that may make all the difference. It may even save their lives.

William Stephenson, PhD

On Falling

My soul conflicts with my fear of dying.

To reduce that fear,
I will seek to know the Great Adventure,
and to trust.

I will choose to pick my life up again
with a new joy.

I will find the courage to wait in the silence
and trust in the darkness.

When the thread of life breaks
and I fall,
underneath are God's everlasting arms.

William Stephenson, PhD

Freedom From Fear

A crisis counseling organization asked me to be a part of a team made up of nine other therapists from around the United States. We would be trained and then sent on a moment's notice to places that had experienced a traumatic event in the community. We were to equip and train those professionals in that community to better assist their citizens who were suffering from traumatic or complicated grief, the fear of it occurring again, the anger and frustration and powerlessness that often comes from an unwanted tragedy.

One such event occurred in the East. For nearly two weeks I worked with those in the community who were specifically dedicated to the children who had been traumatized. The background to this story is that a man had gone into a community center of this small town and killed five people and then himself.

Children were having night terrors. They were afraid of their parents leaving the house for fear they would not come back. They didn't want to go to school or play outside for fear that something would happen to them. Parents and teachers felt powerless in trying to convince many of the children this would not happen again.

I selected seven children who were particularly traumatized. They had all lost someone close to them in the massacre. In an auditorium, I had the children sit on stage in a circle. The auditorium was filled with teachers, social workers, clergy, other children, friends, and family.

I asked the children if they would describe their feelings about the massacre. They were eager to share the anxiety and fear, but they were consistently told by those around them they had nothing to be afraid of. This would not happen to them. Nevertheless, they all described how they couldn't sleep. They were always anxious about being outside. They described waiting for their father and mother to come home and crying if they were late. They were all in grief, and it seemed as if they could not get past that horrible day when someone came into their community center and started killing.

I asked them, *"Do you know who did this?"*

"No," said everyone in the circle.

"Have you ever seen him or a picture of this man?"

And everyone said emphatically, *"No!"*

"How do you feel about this man?"

One boy said, *"I wish I could kill him!"* And others began to express similar feelings. I could see that as they began to express these emotions they were moving out of fear and into anger. Moving out of a non-cognitive position to a cognitive position.

I said, *"I have a picture of the man who did this. Would you let me show it to you?"* They all agreed, and I could sense the anxiety of those in the audience. I put the picture in the middle of the circle so that all the children could see the picture together and at the same time. There was complete silence in the group and in the audience.

After a couple of minutes, I asked the children what they were feeling. One boy said, *"I want to stomp on his face!"*

I said, *"Go ahead. No one will stop you."* And immediately he jumped up and went to the center of the circle and began stomping on the picture and yelling. Soon others got up and began to stomp on the picture and then others until all the children had the opportunity to vent their anger.

Some of the children were crying, but it was a cry of relief. Others began to pace, and some quietly returned to their seats. Those in the audience were also reacting with crying and wanting to come up and support the children.

After everyone had calmed down, I asked, *"Now that you have stomped on his picture, is anyone in the circle feeling afraid?"*

"I'm not afraid anymore. I'm just angry!" And the others agreed.

I turned to the audience of caregivers and supporters of these children and said, *"Now it's your turn. Children have not yet learned how to be afraid and angry at the same time. That part of their brain has not yet developed. But now their fear is gone. Now it's your responsibility to work with these children to move beyond their anger. They are now dealing with this trauma in the present and not out of what could happen. Affirm, don't judge their anger. It's a healthy emotion. Your job is to show them now how they will use their anger to get well again. Good luck."*

I turned to the children and asked if they had anything else to say. And they rushed toward me and gave me a big collective hug. I still hear from some of those children who are now young adults. They still have recall of that tragic moment. But they also remind me they have learned to take back their lives because of that day on a stage in a school auditorium, with a man they saw only a couple of times, but taught them the power of being free from fear.

William Stephenson, PhD

The Consequences of Anger

Not too long ago, divers recovered a German U-boat off Denmark that had been sunk by the Allies in WWII. But it was too dangerous to get close to or to enter because there were still live torpedoes on board capable of blowing up. The war is over, but that German sub is still armed for battle.

I had a client who was a teenager, and he lived in a home like that. Anger flared up. There was a fight, and the home was turned into a battlefield. Then a truce was made. That's all. Just a cessation of hostility. The heat of the anger still smoldered. There was no real reconciliation, no real recovery. There was no true peace restored.

The war was over, but the home was still occupied with live torpedoes. Occupants of the house had to walk gingerly so as not to step on somebody's feelings or else there would be another explosion. And my client asked, *"Dr. Stephenson, what can I do? Where can I go?"*

He was also battling fourth stage cancer. When he died in the hospital, he chose to avoid the dangerous waters by not having his parents with him. I believe he chose not to die in a war zone.

William Stephenson, PhD

The Power of Forgiveness

Randy Johnson was brought into the hospice one day before his 58th birthday. When Randy was admitted, he was angry and hostile, abrupt and extremely restless. When he was asleep, he would moan, as if something terribly wrong had happened.

When asked if everything was okay, he wouldn't answer. The staff knew that he had some unfinished business that he had to deal with if he was to have a "good death."

His physical signs were rapidly deteriorating, but he wouldn't die. He wouldn't let go. It was as if something deep within him would not permit death.

I talked to his son to see if he knew what it was. From the expression on his face, I knew that a family secret was about to be revealed. He said, *"I'm not his only child. He has a daughter in Boston. My dad disowned her nine years ago because she married someone of another race. From his point of view, she had committed the unpardonable sin. He said he would never forgive her."*

I then knew what his unfinished business was all about. I contacted his daughter and urged her to get to the hospice as fast as possible. Several hours later, she arrived.

For the first time in nine years he saw his daughter. He said nothing. He just stared at her.

Then, he opened his arms to his daughter and with all the strength he had left in his life, he hugged her. She brushed away his tears as well as her own. She sat on his bed and neither said anything for the longest time.

Finally, he looked into her eyes and said the words that freed him forever, *"I'm sorry. Please forgive me."*

There were many more tears. They held one another and talked about old times. He learned that he was now a grandfather and there were pictures to see and there was much laughter.

That night, his vital signs were stable and strong. But then an amazing thing began to happen. Around 11:30, he said he was very tired, but he didn't want his children to leave. Each child held one of his hands, and he let go.

The bitterness was gone from his face. All of his unfinished business had been put to rest. It was a good death. I looked at my watch and a new day had begun. It was Sunday. It was Father's Day.

The teachable moment is, we forgive, not for what it does to the person we are struggling to love or forgive, but for what it does for us in forgiving.

How Far?

When I look at some of my relationships,
I'm as far as East is to West!
Endless.

I seem to be remedial
in forgiveness and caring,
but a scholar at what I believe.
Incongruent.

I have mastered communicating
by texting, emailing, and Facebook.
But I'm still struggling with
communication across the dinner table.
Listen.

And I struggle with the "Outsiders."
Surely the ones who don't love God
are outside of the beloved community.
Surely.

But are those I perceive as outsiders,
on the outside?
Really?

Perhaps I will get closer to my soul
if I expand my understanding of community
and include those that God loves as well.
Finally.

William Stephenson, PhD

A Second Look

We need time to sort things out.
To examine the hurts we have
Before we are able to forgive.
It's not an excuse to have time.
It's necessary.

The best thing we can do
For those we love
Who are hurting and broken
And resentful...
Is to not rush in with our solutions
And then become disappointed
When they don't take our advice.

William Stephenson, PhD

But
To enable them to take a second look.
To re-perceive what they are having to deal with.
Because we honor the second look.
We all need a second chance.

Lessons

Remembering the teachers
In my past
Is a time of grace.

So many
Who have gone on before me
Yet still remain
In my cheering section.

I remember
How through their words,
Deeds and capacity,
To listen to me.
Got me unstuck
Again and again.
It is grace
To remember them.

These teachers in my past
Taught me a simple truth
That takes only a moment to say
But has taken a lifetime
For me to learn…
"I cannot have what I will not receive."

William Stephenson, PhD

These teachers in my past
Taught me to trust
As well as to prove.
To open myself to more
Than I wanted to learn.
To be shown more
Than I wanted to see.
To tell me about more
Than I wanted to hear.

These teachers in my past
Who would not give up on me
Continue to cheer me on
To not give up on others.
As I have learned to now sit
In their cheering section
And will remain there
Until they too find their way.

Mitigating Circumstances

They have been married for 45 years, but suddenly it seems as if he has turned into a monster. He can't understand why he is being so hurtful, especially to his wife. He is not sure he will ever be able to forgive himself.

They have been married for 45 years, and suddenly, this man, her husband, is treating her so abusively. She can't understand why. The things he has said and done to her recently are so painful that she doesn't know if she will ever be able to forgive him.

When they came in for counseling, I listened to their story. I asked that they go for a physical examination. And then, together, they hear the doctor use that word for the first time: Alzheimer's.

His hurtful words and abusive behavior didn't hurt any less. However, forgiveness? Now, not only would it be possible, but probable. Now, those 45 years would get them through.

Mitigating circumstances. We just don't know enough, sometimes.

William Stephenson, PhD

Requirements

Some people believe in life after death because
Belief in the JUSTICE of God requires it.
So few feast and so many starve…
That the unfairness of this life is
Somehow balanced out in new life.

Some people believe in life after death because
Belief in the LOVE of God requires it.
At the end of life
We will still have
Expressions of love
That will need to be shared.
There will still be
Songs in our hearts
That will yearn to be sung.

William Stephenson, PhD

Some people believe in life after death because
The MERCY of God requires it.
God has eternity to overcome
The hardest of hearts.

I believe in life after death because
I keep falling in love with people
Again and again.

Love
In the end is not blind.
Love
In the end is the only thing
That puts hope in my eyes.

A Test of Wills

I want to win.
I want to be the first in line.
The first one out.
I want to be the best.

We are told by so many prophets…
"Lording it over other people
And living in the presence of God
Is a contradiction of terms."

Translation…
You can't have peace
And hold on to resentments
At the same time.
No matter how justified and
Righteous the resentment.

Translation…
Insisting on being right
At the expense of someone being wrong
Will never heal a relationship.

William Stephenson, PhD

Solution...
Use the will that we do have
To do God's will!

And so I dare ask,
"What would God's love require
Of me in this situation,
In this relationship?"

Questioning is more important than answers!
Questioning helps me discover
That my problem isn't
That I don't know what to do
Or what the will of God is...

But I discover in questioning
That the real problem is
I don't want to do it!

It's a test of wills!

Grudges

A good memory can be hazardous.
Too often I can recall
Every raised eyebrow,
Every embarrassing moment,
Every slight
Every let-down,
Every put-down.

Then I get tangled up
In guilt and shame.
I get smothered
By my success
And choke
On sobs that nobody cares.

To heal bad memories that are hazardous,
I need to remember
That I'll never heal them
Through revenge.

I will only heal them
By refusing to dwell
On how I've been hurt,
And begin to dwell
On how I've been helped.

I need to stop hiding behind my hurts,
Behind my grudges,
Under tons of disappointment,
Deluged with a list of betrayals.

God just keeps finding me
No matter how I hide,
And when I'm found,
I hear God whisper my name,
Urging me to come out of hiding
And risk trying again.

An Unassembled Peace

I am learning that the peace
God provides
Comes unassembled.
It comes as a do-it-yourself kit.

When in the world
Did we ever get the idea
That God would turn
Our swords into plowshares
And our nuclear warheads
Into bread and milk and medicine
For the poor of the world
By wailing, whining, wishing, wanting?

I am learning that
The peace that God provides
Comes with a paradox.

It is the desire to be a peace lover,
That becomes the biggest barrier
To becoming a peace maker.

There is a problem
And it needs to be dealt with…
Some people are going to be upset.
Some people are going to be hurt.
There's going to be controversy and division.
Pressure to leave some things unsaid,
Remain quiet.
For the love of peace
Of course.

But the problem doesn't go away.
It just keeps building
And finally a postponed explosion occurs,
Often hurting more at the end
Than it would have in the beginning.

Ironic.
The very desire to be a peace lover,
To be peaceable,
To not upset people,
May be the biggest barrier
To being a peace maker.

How can I ever believe otherwise?
I follow the One
Who went to a cross.

I am learning that
My problem with peace
Is not my desire
But my direction.

I am learning that
The peace I want for Israel and the Middle East
Will not come by drones or bombs.

I am learning that
I have more than one option…
In a crisis I get to select how
I am going to react.

Perhaps
The best way to peace
Is for me to confess
That perhaps I need to humbly ask
To be given a new way to travel.

Like Jesus…
Galilee or Jerusalem?

Justification

In a world
In which cruelty is so common,
Anger has to be appropriate.

In a world
In which human solidarity
Is daily proclaimed and hourly betrayed,
Anger is appropriate.

In a world
In which greed rides high, wide and unhandsome,
Leaving many people out
Of God's gifts of plenty…
Anger is appropriate.

In this kind of world,
The absence of anger
Is the essence of evil.

William Stephenson, PhD

An Awakened Soul

As I begin this day
I am awakened to my soul
And I am grateful
For the common, familiar
And miraculous things.
For the good earth beneath my feet,
For the stately clouds above my head,
For the beauty of memories nestled in my heart.

As I begin this day,
I awaken my soul no less
For all frightened lives, boldly lived.
For handicapped lives, courageously lived,
For all shortened lives, faithfully lived.

William Stephenson, PhD

As I begin this day
I awaken my soul
Lest I forget
That from day to day
And moment to moment,
My life has been blessed
And my experience enriched
By those who have gone on before me.

As I begin this day
My soul is awake
So that I don't become obsessed
With what I lack
Lest I rob my soul of joy
For all I have.

Free to Believe

Too often
I get bound up
In beliefs and doctrines
That I really don't believe.
Giving lip service
To petty religious beliefs
That I know
Are not ultimately important,
But using them to
Compare myself favorably with others.
They believe in them
So I guess I should too!

Too often
I have made "deals" with God…
"Business transactions."
Saying that
If God does this for me
I'll do this for God!
As if
I have my own modern day
Practice of indulgences!

Too often
I have exhausted
My time of searching my soul
Examining my past
Dwelling on my misdeeds
Examining my dark side.
Hoping that I can find peace
In the present
By delving into the
Black hole of my past.

But then
Comes this freedom
Of belief that says,

"Forget trying to achieve
Your own salvation.
You'll never make it!
You'll just end up
In either despair
Or in arrogance!
Accept
Your life as a gift
From God,
And rejoice in it!
Trust
In what God has done
For you
And you'll be free.
Free
To be human,
To love,
To let other people love you.
Free
At last!
To discover your one true self
And to enjoy the life
That God has given you."

And then
My journey of wholeness
Will begin anew.

My Resource

As I begin this new day,
my soul waits for God
to come gently into my life
like the fading of dark and daybreak.

I yearn to awaken
all the resources of my faith,
lest I measure my hope
by the mood of the moment,
and miss what this new day
has in store for me.

As I begin this new day,
I now open myself to this gentleness,
reminding myself
that God is already within me.

As I accept this gentle strength
I am then able to have the wisdom
to share.

William Stephenson, PhD

As My Day Begins

As my day begins,
  I will learn to grow
    into my commitments.

  So
      they will be too strong
        to tolerate injustice in my thinking.

  So
    I will be too honest
      to tamper with truth in my loving.

  So
    I will be too helpful
      to be lenient with evil.

As my day begins
  I will seek to have
    an inner balance.

So
  I will forever outweigh forgiveness to the
    blame that I have cast on others.

So
  I save the sharpest
    thrust of conscience for myself.

So
  there will be
    no malice, bitterness, or revenge left in me.

Beginnings

Let this new beginning into recovery
Be a time to re-sensitize my vision.
To give me rest and renewal.
To be refreshed and know
That I can begin again.
To be touched and felt with the
Forgiveness that I can embrace.

As I live through this new beginning
Let me fight off any self-pity in my loss,
Any fear of what is to come.

Let the legacy of my memories
Of having been loved
Speak through my actions
Of goodwill and caring for others.

To embrace the challenge to be open,
To change, and to tomorrow,
And to reach out to others
With the quiet and confidence of faith.

To not add to the hopelessness
Of anyone that comes in my midst.

I will live with what I
Embrace in this new beginning.
To touch others with God's grace
And be glad.

William Stephenson, PhD

On Finishing

As I come to a new place in my life
I know that the theme
Is beginning again
Or,
Starting over.

However,
The older I get
The longer I live
I yearn for ways to finish things
I've already started!

There are doors
I've knocked on
For a long time,
And walls I'd like to get over.

Sometimes
My desire for starting over
Is really a cover-up,
A smoke-screen
For difficult decisions
I don't want to make or face.

I need hope.
A reminder
That God will never place me
In a room where all the doors
Are permanently locked
Or where all the walls
Are insurmountable.

William Stephenson, PhD

As I journey into this new beginning
I need breakthroughs!
I need innovation!

I don't need cynics and critics.
I need people in my life
Who are door-openers
And wall-leapers.

And so
I begin again,
And I sigh...
Because I now know that
I cannot expect
The strength or resources
I pray to have
Until I first step into the water.

A Need For An Ending

When a story or a relationship has an ending
It says that life makes sense.

When a story or a relationship has an ending
It says that life is going somewhere.

When a story or a relationship has an ending
It says to us that how we live our life,
The quality of our life
Is going to make a difference.

We need to know that our lives
Will count for something.

We need to know that living for what is right
Is going to make a difference.

William Stephenson, PhD

We need to know that being moral
Is rooted in the foundation of the universe
And that it's not just right for me
But it's eternally right forever and ever.

I need to know that my sense of goodness
Is supported, not rewarded.

I need to know that the universe
Is on my side and that evil
Ultimately will fail.

There is a need for an ending
So that we will have the courage
To go on with the present.

There is a need for an ending
So that we will have hope
For the future.

There is a need for an ending
So that what we hope for,
For ourselves and for our loved ones,
Is going to be vindicated.

There is a need for an ending
So that we know that
That which is good
But seems in peril now, will survive.
And what is incomplete now
Is going to be fulfilled then.

Every journey,
Spiritual or relational,
Needs an ending.

And then
Hopefully,
A new beginning…

An Epilogue:
The Storyteller

I had known Barry and Marian before they married. We went to the same church and our friendships were also intermingled. They were a wonderful couple and when they decided to marry, most of the church attended.

Marian became pregnant almost immediately. She would be a fantastic mother because of her upbringing. Barry was scared to death.

But then Mary came into their lives and Barry became an incredible loving father. He doted over his daughter. Seeing them in church together was reason enough to be there.

Our church had in its worship service a time for children to come forward and listen to a story that spoke of this man called Jesus. The pastor knew that in the facility I was working, there was a ward for children who were fighting for their lives. She also witnessed times when at the end of the day we would bring the children into the recreation room and end the day with them all around me on this huge circle rug and I would proceed to tell them a story.

Our pastor would on occasion invite me to be the storyteller for the children during the service. It was such a celebration to watch them come running down the aisles, all hoping to get as close to me as they could. And Mary, she was one of the fastest and always found a way to sit up next to me every time. She had a smile that could break your heart.

One Sunday, after finishing my story, Mary stood up and said,

> *"Dr. Bill, my mom says that all your stories have a 'chapter two.' I don't know what that means but she says there's more to tell us in your stories. Would you tell us more about this girl next time?"*

I had been found out by an eight-year-old. I stuttered and stammered and finally, I said, *"Mary, I promise to tell you the end of this story next time. But I don't know when that'll be."*

"Next Sunday!" the pastor announced. And the kids all cheered and gave Mary high fives.

But Mary would not hear "chapter two." None of the children would hear "chapter two." Mary fainted in school that week and she was rushed to the hospital for a series of tests. The blood tests revealed a very ominous story. Leukemia and the worst kind. The prognosis would become a nightmare of treatment and heartache. This would be Mary's "chapter two." I would become her therapist as well as to her parents, Marian and Barry.

Mary's leukemia spread very quickly and this was a time when we didn't have medical treatment for this disease that we have now. Furthermore, one of the treatments for this disease was quarantine. Whenever Mary was home, she couldn't go outside and could only have family members visit with her. Her friends could not come into visit and were relegated to sitting on the outside of the sliding glass door and Mary sitting on the inside, usually on the lap of her dad, Barry.

Their church participation also ended very abruptly. It all ended when Mary asked me about "chapter two." But the particular pew the three of them sat was conspicuously empty Sunday after Sunday.

Mary died within four months of her diagnosis. It felt like a disaster had struck our community. I continued to provide Marian and Barry counseling but the grief was so widespread that it seemed as if the whole church was in need of grief counseling. Even the children's moments in the service were put on hold because no one would volunteer. It seemed as if the joy that we cherished in our services was now absent.

In time the Children's Moments returned to the order of worship and periodically I was asked to be the lead. While others would read something to the children, I would always tell a story that had a message of hope and purpose. And as before, the children raced down the aisles to get close to me as they could. Except for two times they attended, Marian and Barry remained absent. Both of those times I was the storyteller in the service.

They were now alone and isolated with their grief, with their pain. And ironically, the church also seemed to be isolated with their grief. One could almost sense that a cloud was hanging over our church. Some even confessed that they felt relief when they came to church and Marian and Barry weren't there. *"What do I say?" "I dread facing them!"*

But Marian and Barry remained committed to the counseling. I could see that they were making progress. In one of our last counseling sessions, I asked Marian and Barry about their absence in church. Marian said,

> *"It's the Children's Moments we can't handle. Especially when you are asked to share a story with the children. We see the children running down the aisle so that they can be closest to you, just as Mary did, and we go to pieces. And you don't make it any better because of the kind of stories you tell and the way you tell them. We're nearly sobbing and everyone around us feel so helpless."*

We looked at each other for the longest time and finally I responded.

> *"Marian, perhaps it hurts so bad because you and Barry have a story that needs to be told. Not just to the children, but there's a whole congregation that needs to hear it. You two need to tell your story because it's a story of hope. It's a story of love and faith found in your marriage and a community called the church. Would you be willing to join me and share your story of hope? To share in the weeks to come how hard it is to hope when life seems to be crashing down upon you. It's the "second chapter" that Mary hopes you will tell to others needing a word of hope."*

You could almost see a light turn on over Marian's head as she said,

> *"Bill, you think she's there in the children's moments, don't you. When you tell a story you sense that she's sitting right beside you and that's why you are asking me to help with the children because she's there! Am I right?"*

Again, a long period of silence. When she realized I wasn't going to give her an answer, she said,

> *"Alright, I'll do it! When shall we start?"*

"Next Sunday!" I said with raised voice, mimicking our pastor.

It wasn't long before Marian became the most popular storyteller in the church. She was a natural. She had those kids mesmerized. And she would always find a way to include Mary, the one child she truly believed was also in that circle.

Barry also became a storyteller. He was invited to speak before several service organizations where he eloquently told his story of the father of a child, dying, and how his faith in his relationships kept him afloat. Especially with his wife.

But other changes began to occur. From out of nowhere came a weekly meeting of a new group for mothers who had experienced the loss of a child. Some of the women who attended had no loss to share but came because the group was so honest and safe.

Even our pastor got caught up in this new spirit. She moved the singing of the Doxology from after the offering to when the children were leaving the Children's Moments and exited to their Sunday School classes. They left the sanctuary every Sunday, hearing the congregation sing,

> Praise God, from whom all blessings flow,
> Praise God, all creatures here below;
> Praise God, above the heavenly host;
> Praise Father, Son and Holy Ghost. Amen.

One Sunday, Marian was able to say after we had told a story to the children together and the congregation was singing the Doxology with unusual enthusiasm,

"That's where my Mary is, Bill. She's with the heavenly Host."

She was not alone. The congregation embraced a new hope or perhaps it was a new hope that embraced them. Indeed.

It is at this point in this story that I would expect Mary to stand up and say, *"Dr. Bill, will you tell us the "second chapter" to this story?"*

Marian and Barry would have another daughter, who now begins college this year. But she has also become a storyteller with such skill and imagination that the whole sanctuary is silent when she tells a story to the children. She credits her skill from the inspiration of her mother, Marian, and to her sister, Mary, whom she never knew. **Chapter two.**

www.ingramcontent.com/pod-product-compliance
Lightning Source LLC
LaVergne TN
LVHW041841070526
838199LV00045BA/1391